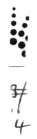

$\frac{37}{4}$

THE LAST DAYS OF TROY

# The Last Days of Troy

SIMON ARMITAGE

FABER & FABER

First published in 2014
by Faber & Faber Ltd
Bloomsbury House
74–77 Great Russell Street
London WC1B 3DA

Typeset by Country Setting, Kingsdown, Kent CT14 8ES
Printed in England by Martins the Printers, Berwick-upon-Tweed

A CIP record for this book
is available from the British Library

ISBN 978–0–571–31509–3

FSC
www.fsc.org
MIX
Paper from
responsible sources
FSC® C101712

10 9 8 7 6 5 4 3 2 1

Homer's epic poem the *Iliad*, written around 700 BCE, begins in the final year of the Trojan War. Led by Agamemnon, a loose alliance of Greek forces has sailed across the Aegean Sea to bring home Helen, the wife of Menelaus, abducted or seduced by Paris and now living as his wife or concubine within the walled city of Ilium, in the region of Troy. But after almost a decade, an end to the war is nowhere in sight. Infighting and personal enmity between the Greek leaders is threatening to split the coalition apart. Within the besieged city, Trojans are haunted not only by the idea of defeat but by the potential destruction of their civilisation. Even the Gods on Olympus are squabbling among themselves, their favouritism and interventions only prolonging the conflict and exacerbating the misery.

Rather than chronicle the entire war, Homer chose to concentrate on a relatively short period of time – about fifty days – and to focus on relationships and interactions between leading characters on both sides. Yes, there are big battles, but essentially his is a story which takes us behind the scenes, to what goes on in the tents, corridors, halls and chambers, and beyond the clouds. After some 15,000 lines, the *Iliad* comes to its enigmatic and poetic conclusion, but at that point we are still no nearer finding out what happened to its leading characters, or who won the war. Some of this information comes to light subsequently through other sources, including Homer's *Odyssey*, in which we are told for the first time how Greek soldiers were smuggled through the impenetrable gates in a wooden horse. But the subject of the last days of Troy is taken up most compellingly by the Roman poet Virgil, over six hundred years later. In Book II of his *Aeneid*, through the voice of Aeneas, a survivor from Troy, we are given a graphic and intense account of those final hours and of the bloody fates of the defeated. My aim in this dramatisation has been to span those two ancient poems, and present in theatrical form a story that follows the Trojan War through to its bitter end.

The play opens in modern day Hisarlik on the tip of north-west Turkey, the archaeological site of what is widely considered to be the actual geographical location of Troy. To visit the dusty ruins and crumbling walls is to suffer a confusion of information and to experience a tug of war between the heart and the head. Legend and artefact coexist here; fact and fantasy mingle and blur, to the point where it's impossible to say where history ends and mythology begins. In relation to the Trojan War this is as true today as it was for Homer, who was writing about events said to have taken place in the Bronze Age, four or five hundred years before he was born. Indeed, even Homer's authorship and his very existence are by no means universally accepted. We are dealing with a mystery that has come to us in echoes and whispers from over three thousand years ago.

Ancient fables endure for all kinds of reasons, but their continued relevance to the way we live now plays a major part in their survival. At the time when this play will be premiered, many countries will be marking and commemorating the centenary of the First World War, with images of atrocities and questions of military morality high in people's minds, just as they were for Homer. Moreover, the channel or strait that runs from the Bosphorus to the Dardanelles or Hellespont continues to symbolise a political, economic, cultural, philosophical and religious fault line between east and west. In that context, the story of Troy is a blueprint for a conflict that rages to this day. Homer was also astute enough to know that although it is armies who go to war it is usually the individual psychologies of their leaders that send their people into battle. Prejudice, pigheadedness, petulance or just a momentary whim can result in the slaughter of millions. Nothing has changed.

If Helen is said to be the face that launched a thousand ships, and if each Greek vessel was crewed by up to two hundred men, and if the Trojan forces were equal in number, as they must have been to ensure a reasonably fair fight, then as well as reducing ten years' worth of backstory to two or three hours of performance, I was also faced with the task of reducing over four hundred thousand participants to a cast of about a dozen. So a whole pantheon of gods, with their various allegiances and attributes, are represented through Zeus, Hera and Athene. On the ground, minor characters, parallel narratives and self-contained episodes have been omitted, and some principal characters rolled into one. Odysseus, for example, is an amalgamation of several high-ranking nobles in the Greek encampment, though he still retains (I hope) those personal traits forever associated with him. But challenges often present unanticipated opportunities: Menelaus is an important figure in the original story, but as the play developed I found his absence to be a more useful dramatic device than his presence. His brother, Agamemnon, must do his bidding, just as the whole Greek army must sail to war on behalf of a cuckold. Other characters and scenes have grown in relation to their original status. Helen, little more than a walk-on part in Homer's poem, is pivotal to this version. And at one point I require several thousand Trojan soldiers to surge across no-man's-land, a problem I have left at the door of the director.

*The Last Days of Troy* was commissioned by the Royal Exchange Theatre, Manchester, for production in spring 2014. Further performances were then scheduled at Shakespeare's Globe in London via a full stage transfer. Ten years ago I dramatised Homer's *Odyssey* for BBC radio. It had always been my intention to attempt something similar with its counterpart, a 'prequel' as it might be labelled and packaged these days, and I'm genuinely grateful for the opportunity. I'd like to thank Sarah Frankom, Artistic Director at the

Royal Exchange, for opening up discussions, for her initial responses and ongoing ideas, and for creating the conditions under which this piece could develop. It's oddly satisfying to remember that an ambitious dramatisation of the first work of Western literature and one of the greatest poems in the history of the world should have been plotted in the café of Hebden Bridge railway station. Thanks are also due to all other staff at the Exchange for their support and expertise, to the numerous actors who took part in workshops and read-throughs, to Dominic Dromgoole at the Globe for his expressions of enthusiasm, to Sue Roberts, to Glyn Maxwell, and to everyone else who read the script with an open mind and editorial eye during its evolution. Finally, enormous thanks to director Nick Bagnall, who was attached to the project from its abstract beginnings, and whose conversation and good company are woven into the text. Writing is essentially an antisocial occupation; it is both a relief and a privilege to collaborate and to work with people who turn matchsticks into boats, plastic stones into citadels, hot air into enormous horses and words into people.

SIMON ARMITAGE

# THE LAST DAYS OF TROY

## CHARACTERS

### The Greeks

AGAMEMNON, commander of the Greek forces
ODYSSEUS, a high-ranking captain
ACHILLES, a noble warrior
PATROCLUS, Achilles' compatriot and comrade
SINON, a soldier
HELEN, wife of Agamemnon's brother, Menelaus, seduced
    by Paris

### The Trojans

PRIAM, King of Troy
HECTOR, Priam's son, a warrior, leader of the Trojan forces
ANDROMACHE, Hector's wife
ASTYANAX, Hector and Andromache's young boy
PARIS, Priam's other son
BRISEIS, a local girl captured by the Greeks, Achilles' lover

### The Gods

ZEUS, the Almighty, father of the skies, and a present-day
    pedlar
HERA, his wife
ATHENE, Zeus' daughter
THETIS, a sea-nymph, mother of Achilles

Zeus and Hera are both gods of the ancient past and contemporary
characters, and are played by the same actors. Their character names
appear in small capitals (ZEUS and HERA) when speaking or appearing
as ancient gods and in bold italic (*Zeus* and *Hera*) in the present day.

# ACT ONE

# Bristol Central Library

Tel: 0117 9037200

www.bristol.gov.uk/libraries

## Self Payment 22/01/2016 14:13

XXXXXX8062

Amount Tendered: £2.10

Amount Paid: £2.10

**Amount Outstanding: £0.00**

Thank you for using self-service at
Bristol Libraries.

## SCENE ONE

*Present-day Troy, the archaeological and tourist site of*
*Hisarlik, Turkey.*

*Spray-painted in gold and impersonating a statue, Zeus*
*stands on a wooden box with a collection tin at his feet*
*and a sign saying* ZEUS. *Behind him, on his small cart, are*
*souvenirs and trinkets from the story of the* Iliad, *including*
*action figures in the shape of Achilles, Agamemnon, Priam*
*et al.*

**Zeus**
Fury.

RAGE!

Goddess of memory,
draw from my throat
the story of Achilles, son of Peleus,
whose wounded pride
brought suffering and misery
to his own comrades,
sent the souls of warriors
to the land of the dead
till the battlefields of Troy
were scarlet with blood, and by day
crows scavenged
on lips and eyes, and at night
dogs feasted on the limbs and innards
of lifeless bodies beneath the stars,
all under the watch
of almighty Zeus.

Conjure in my mind the moment it began,
when words flew between brothers in arms,
and a feud was born.

*Tired and unappreciated, he steps down from the box and takes a drink from a bottle of water. Once rested, he goes to the cart and picks up a few of the action figures, staring at them, considering them, then begins to arrange them on the box, like a boy playing with toy soldiers.*

### Zeus

Ten years into this most gruelling of military confrontations and we're still no closer to any kind of resolution. A decade ago, leaders and warlords from almost every kingdom in Greece mobilised a task force of thousands of men, sailed east, pitched camp on the shore and laid siege to the walled city of Troy on the far bank of the Scamander River. Motive: vengeance. Objective: return Helen to her rightful country and lawful husband. Progress thus far: nil. Current situation: stalemate, with neither Greeks nor Trojans prepared to surrender an inch of ground or contemplate defeat. On one side, under Agamemnon's command, conditions in the Greek base are squalid and the morale of homesick and weary men impossible to judge. On the other side resources are running low and nerves are threadbare in King Priam's besieged citadel. It's hard to see this concluding without some all-out catastrophic battle, an endgame or finale, like a great storm that clears the air, and when it comes may the gods have pity on those who hear its thunder. But until that time dark clouds mass overhead. The immovable object holds firm against the irresistible force, and this terrible war drags on. And on.

## SCENE TWO

*The ancient past. The Greek encampment on the shores of*
*Troy. Agamemnon's tent. Agamemnon is studying maps of*
*the campaign. Odysseus enters.*

AGAMEMNON
Say something positive or say nothing at all.

*Odysseus doesn't respond.*

AGAMEMNON
Speak!

ODYSSEUS
Worse than yesterday. Disease . . . fever. First the dogs,
now the horses. Open wounds to the flesh – every
morning it's as if a rain of arrows has fallen on the
camp. The men too – blisters, sores, lethargy . . .

AGAMEMNON
Bellyaching. Skiving.

ODYSSEUS
I've looked in their eyes. It's genuine illness.

AGAMEMNON
Homesickness and fatigue, whining and malingering,
and you've fallen for it, Odysseus, you of all people,
wise and cunning.

ODYSSEUS
It's correct that I know an untruth when I see one,
Agamemnon. My lord.

*Enter Achilles and Patroclus.*

AGAMEMNON

See how they breeze in here unannounced. There's no discipline.

PATROCLUS

We agreed to an assembly, to discuss this crisis.

AGAMEMNON

There's no crisis and there's no assembly. If you'll excuse me, I have battle plans to study. Strategy, tactics . . .

ACHILLES

It's a plague.

AGAMEMNON

Ah, Achilles, come straight to the point, why bother constructing a case based on evidence and rational thought. Just blurt it out, be my guest.

PATROCLUS

Listen to Achilles.

AGAMEMNON

Gossip. Superstition – that's the only contagion around here, and now he's dignified it with a name and delivered it into my ears hoping to infect me with it too.

ACHILLES

Gossip never made a horse chew off its own tongue and its eyes pop out of its head, did it? Gossip never made a man cough up black blood or become a corpse in his bed overnight. We can't bury them fast enough – some men are digging their own graves.

PATROCLUS

We've consulted Calchas.

AGAMEMNON

Give me strength. That old fishwife!

PATROCLUS

He examined the entrails of a slaughtered goat.

AGAMEMNON

Of course he did. How else to predict the future!

ODYSSEUS

He's never been wrong.

AGAMEMNON

He's never said a good word on my behalf. (*Pause*) So go on then, tell me what the future holds according to the all-seeing, all-knowing visionary Calchas.

PATROCLUS

It's because of the girl you took, the one with the dark skin. The priest's daughter. Every day he stands outside your tent offering treasure and ransom, begging for her return, but you flatly refuse him. You insult the priest of Apollo, so Apollo sends a plague, and won't relent until you give up the girl. That is the prophecy of Calchas.

AGAMEMNON

He's a doom-monger – he loves it, like a dog rolling around in other dogs' shit. One day he's a dealer in hearsay, a tittle-tattler, the next he's a prophet for my whole army, telling me, Agamemnon, to give up what I won in battle. She's mine. In fact I prefer her to my wife. Just as attractive, very skilful with her hands, if not more so. She's mine by right.

ODYSSEUS

Agamemnon . . .

AGAMEMNON

Though if it soothes troubled minds and calms tender nerves, of course I can give her up. I'm capable of that.

ACHILLES
Then it's settled.

AGAMEMNON
But I demand another prize in her place. Otherwise I'll
be the only one among us to have lost out, and where's
the fairness in that?

ACHILLES
Unrivalled Agamemnon, greediest of them all. Where
will the Greeks find you another reward?

AGAMEMNON
For such a renowned swordsman you have a blunt and
clumsy tongue, Achilles.

ACHILLES
What we took from ransacked towns has been shared
out – are you suggesting we ask for donations on your
behalf?

AGAMEMNON
I won't be hoodwinked by you, tricked into giving up
my bounty while you cling to your own.

ACHILLES
Just do what the gods insist and give the girl back, and
once we've conquered Troy there'll be more treasure
than even you can stuff into the lining of your coat.

AGAMEMNON
Bring me something as compensation, or I'll take what
I choose.

ACHILLES
You arrogant pig.

ODYSSEUS
Gentlemen, let's keep this dignified.

ACHILLES

Why men fight for you I've no idea. *I've* no quarrel with
these Trojans – there's a wide sea and a tall mountain to
keep us apart.

AGAMEMNON

You're a mercenary – you'd start a fight in an empty
field.

ACHILLES

I sailed to Troy as a favour to you, because your brother
wasn't man enough for his own wife.

AGAMEMNON

Abduction!

ACHILLES

And while my brave Myrmidons fight your battles, you
sit on your cushioned behind dividing the spoils of war,
raking the lion's share into your own lap and throwing
the loose change in the direction of others. I might as
well set sail right now.

AGAMEMNON

Go! I need nothing from you, especially not your
jealousy and tantrums. And take your precious
Myrmidons with you – there'll be more respect without
that mutinous provincial rabble, and less mouths to
feed, and less grabbing hands when it comes to sharing
out the rewards of victory.

ACHILLES

You'll be obliterated in a week.

AGAMEMNON

And another thing. That girl I've seen you with, the one
with the painted fingernails and toes.

PATROCLUS
  Briseis belongs to Achilles, he won her in battle.

AGAMEMNON
  I'll take *her* as my prize, since you're robbing me of my
  own. Let it be known she's to become mine; then no one
  will be in any doubt about who stands tallest among us,
  and even you might learn some respect, soldier.

ACHILLES
  You're a mongrel-faced coward, and a drunk one at that.

AGAMEMNON
  You're a common murderer. A terrorist!

ACHILLES
  When he hears the battle-cry he pisses himself with fear.

AGAMEMNON
  The gods put a spear in his fist and he's never been able
  to let go.

ODYSSEUS
  Agamemnon, don't take the girl from him – you don't
  need her. And Achilles, you have a goddess for a mother
  but Agamemnon, by the authority of Zeus, rules over
  many people – honour him from that.

ACHILLES
  Those he rules over are blind or stupid, how else could
  they love such a sly lumbering creature, bloated by praise?

AGAMEMNON
  You'll learn some manners.

*They are about to square up to each other when Patroclus
and Odysseus intervene.*

ACHILLES

Your own army presented me with the girl and now
you scrounge her back – let that be Agamemnon's way.
But I'll take no more orders from you and you'll take
nothing else from me. Not a coin or a cup, not a grain
or a grape. Come near me again, and I'll show every one
of these Greeks that the blood of their great leader runs
pink and thin.

*Achilles and Patroclus leave.*

AGAMEMNON (*to Odysseus*)

Tell every man to bathe and purify himself and throw
the dirty water in the sea. Have the whole camp tidied
and swept, till there isn't a flea still breathing. Once the
vermin are cleared, sacrifice bulls and goats.

Then go to Achilles' tent and bring me the girl. If he
refuses, have her dragged out, with him clinging to her
ankles if that's what it takes.

## SCENE THREE

*A sunlit upper room within the walled city of Troy. Helen is working at a long-by-narrow tapestry. Enter Andromache.*

ANDROMACHE
This is where you're hiding. Paris is looking for you.

HELEN
He knows where to find me.

ANDROMACHE
Yes, always here in this room, always stitching. What is it anyway, some kind of map or story?

HELEN
It speaks for itself, doesn't it?

ANDROMACHE
Yes it speaks, like the woman who makes it, but what does it say?

HELEN
Greeks here.

ANDROMACHE
With their long hair and dark ships, camped on the beach.

HELEN
Trojans here.

ANDROMACHE
Glittering Troy.

HELEN
And war in between.

ANDROMACHE

Here's a man skewering a man through the lungs with a spear, and the guts spilling out. And someone sliced in half by a chariot wheel. You have an eye for detail, no doubt about that.

HELEN

Ten years a student, and a grandstand view.

ANDROMACHE (*pointing at the tapestry*)

Is this me? It *is* me, isn't it, in the blue dress. Holding Astyanax – I like the cute smile you've stitched on his little face. And Hector standing behind. Why is his sword drawn?

HELEN

Protection. Love?

ANDROMACHE

And none of your business, actually. But where are you in all this? Where's Helen?

HELEN

It's unfinished.

ANDROMACHE

Of course, how could it be complete without the world's most beautiful woman since the beginning of time?

HELEN

So where would you position me?

ANDROMACHE

If we Trojans win you'll be here, a princess of Troy, my sister-in-law, blowing kisses from the balcony on to the jubilant crowd below. If the Greeks triumph you'll be over there, the rescued queen, carried home on a float,

showered with jasmine and myrtle. Wearing my jewels
I suppose.

HELEN

Was Paris really asking for me, or is this you, out
hunting?

ANDROMACHE

I know exactly where you fit in: on the arm of whichever
man gives the victory speech, and with a cemetery in the
background, downwind.

HELEN

I was a wife in Greece, now I'm a wife in Troy.

ANDROMACHE

You've been sleeping with men since the age of ten – that
much is well known.

HELEN

I was raped on a riverbank. There was no sleep.

ANDROMACHE

You'll do anything a man asks, that's why they're all
cuckoo for you.

HELEN

No man has ever *asked* me for anything.

*Andromache goes towards the door, then turns and comes
back.*

ANDROMACHE

When you walk in a room the men smell sex, the women
smell death.

HELEN

No, the women smell sex – that's why they detest me.
The men smell death, and it smells exciting, because it
smells like war. They smell meat, blood.

ANDROMACHE

You bring out something bitter and vulgar in me.

HELEN

You're a good woman, Andromache. Married to a good
man. The tapestry says as much, doesn't it. Just frightened.
Fear, that's your scent.

*Pause. Andromache lifts Helen's arm and remarks on her
skin.*

ANDROMACHE

Ivory? Pearl? No, whiter than that. Whiter than white.
There wasn't enough whiteness in the known world to
stitch her into this scene – that's what they'll say. Not in
the whitest lead, not in sugar or chalk, not in moonlit
water, in the crocus, the lily, in all the snow on the peak
of Olympus . . . Delicate. Brittle. White-faced Helen
behind her white veil. Wedded to Troy, wearing her
wedding dress? Or in mourning for Greece?

HELEN

I come from Sparta where the soil is red.

ANDROMACHE

The soil is red wherever you walk, wherever you lie down.

The family are waiting to eat. Go to the table. Sit at
your husband's side.

*After a pause, Helen exits. Andromache examines the
tapestry, then follows.*

## SCENE FOUR

*Achilles' tent. Both on their knees next to the bed, Achilles is holding Briseis, whispering to her. At the door, Patroclus draws his sword.*

PATROCLUS (*to Achilles*)
Odysseus approaches, with armed men.

ACHILLES
Let him in.

*Enter Odysseus.*

ODYSSEUS
I'm embarrassed to be here.

ACHILLES
It's your duty. I've no argument with you.

ODYSSEUS
Your conversation with Agamemnon took a wrong turn. You both said things you didn't mean. This can be resolved.

ACHILLES
Take her. Give her to him.

*Briseis begins to sob.*

PATROCLUS
Achilles, there's no greater insult. If it were a gold crown or a silver necklace – that would be bad enough. But to take this woman who shares your bed – who I know you care for – and to think of his hands, and his greedy eyes and his foul breath . . .

ACHILLES
Enough, Patroclus.

*Achilles raises Briseis to her feet, whispering again in her
ear as she sobs and clings to him, then lifts her into his
arms and passes her over to Odysseus.*

ACHILLES
Now leave me.

*Odysseus exits, carrying Briseis.*

PATROCLUS
Achilles . . .

ACHILLES
Go.

*Exit Patroclus. Achilles wanders around the tent, sits on
the bed. From a brush on a table he draws out a strand of
hair.*

ACHILLES
A man born under a pomegranate tree
with its trailing ribbons and skirt of leaves
and baubles crammed with flesh-coloured beads
becomes weak and laughable under its shade,

just reaching up whenever he likes
to fill his belly and quench his thirst,
a pitiful creature with sticky fingers,
with juice in his beard and a smile full of seeds.

Well, the son of a goddess might grow up the same:
squealing out prayers, raising his arms,
demanding that every wrong be put right –
every toothache eased, every nosebleed staunched,
every broken bone to be healed overnight,

every bird in the canopy singing his fame,
every star in the galaxy spelling his name.

*The son of a goddess could fall over backwards*
*talking to clouds, imploring a goddess to intervene.*

*My unearthly mother, have I called on you once?*
*In fury or agony, love or war?*
*Have I ever begged, have you ever heard*
*a whispered appeal, a mumbled request?*
*Not a word. Not one solitary word. Because*
*nothing was offered, so nothing was asked.*

*But I ask now. Lay Agamemnon low.*
*I was born for this battle, this war of all wars;*
*instead I'm diminished, belittled, made small.*
*He dishonours my name – drags it through foreign mud –*
*and to blacken my name is to blacken yours,*
*which is blasphemy, which is sacrilege.*

*So breathe now in the ear of Zeus.*
*Make the Greeks suffer till the king of the Greeks*
*comes crown in hand, on bended knee,*
*grovelling for help, kissing my feet.*

*Punish Agamemnon*
*and love your son.*

## SCENE FIVE

*Olympus. Zeus is standing over a table with a large map laid across it. The other gods are to one side helping themselves to food and drink.*

*Zeus, like a croupier, is moving shapes and objects around the map.*

ZEUS

Rain here, to swell the streams and nourish the vines. A warm wind here to dry the sails of the ships and the fishing nets. Thunderstorms here, here and here – let Zeus be heard. (*To the other gods*) Quiet please, while I work. Snow to this peak, along this ridge, snow to these mountain slopes. Mist over this plain, dew on the leaves at dawn. A rainbow. A visitor – I see you, Thetis, in the corner of my eye.

THETIS

As Zeus sees everyone and everywhere. There's nowhere to hide.

ZEUS

No hiding a woman's intention. You're here with a favour to ask.

THETIS

Father of the skies, in action and in speech, haven't I always put you first?

ZEUS

It begins with the buttering up, and sweet honey straight from the honeycomb. Then comes the knife.

THETIS

Sir, honour my son, that's my request.

ZEUS
　　Well, I expected a little more honey than that, I have
　　to say.

THETIS
　　You know Achilles' fate as well as I do: to die young, an
　　early death. Have I ever pleaded otherwise? But why
　　should he suffer while his life lasts? Agamemnon abuses
　　and humiliates him, takes away his prize. It's a violation.
　　So I ask, let the Trojans enjoy success in battle, until the
　　Greeks go to my son and beg him to come back.

ZEUS
　　Thetis, my dear Thetis . . .

THETIS
　　Zeus, you won't have forgotten how I saved you once,
　　when those gods who now kiss your hand and bow to
　　your every whim plotted against you, had you bound in
　　chains, and I alone summoned help, risked my own
　　neck. Am I not owed something for that?

*Zeus is silent while he ponders. Thetis comes closer to him,
puts her hand against his cheek.*

　　Do I need to embarrass myself to get you to say yes?

ZEUS
　　I'll get grief for this. If my wife Hera sees us together –
　　she already thinks I side with the Trojans and barks out
　　her complaints in front of the other gods – but leave me
　　now, I'll do what I can.

THETIS
　　When Zeus makes a binding promise he signals it with
　　the nod of his head, which all the gods recognise and
　　respect. Do you bow your head? Zeus, do you bow your
　　head?

*Zeus bows his head. There is a roll of thunder. Thetis withdraws.*

HERA

I saw that.

ZEUS

What did you see, my darling?

HERA

Scheming and conniving behind my back, hatching plots. Why am I never consulted?

ZEUS

Hera, I wouldn't trouble you with the burdens of my mind, it wouldn't be fair. And when Zeus does see fit to tell the world of his decisions, you're always the first to hear.

HERA

You paint me as the nagging spouse. You're the supreme god and you'll do whatever you like, that's understood. But when I see Thetis winding you around her little finger it makes me think she's sweet-talked you into favouring her precious son Achilles and bringing hurt and degradation to the noble Greeks at the same time. Do I imagine correctly?

ZEUS

Your imagination is to be applauded. But your insolence *is not*. Accept my judgement in these matters and stand in silence, or let the other gods be witnesses to hurt and degradation closer to home. Is *that* understood?

HERA

You overbearing tyrant . . .

ATHENE (*intervening*)

No, really, please. Bickering over mere mortals? Carry on like this and there'll be threats, sulking, vengeance –

shouldn't we leave all that to humankind and rise above it? Let's enjoy the food while it's fresh! (*Aside, to Hera.*) Don't push him too far, he'll thrash you or pick you up by the foot and sling you from Olympus. (*To all, circulating with a jug.*) So let's drink. Everyone, lift up your cups and raise a glass to almighty Zeus.

ALL (*toasting*)
Almighty Zeus.

*While the other gods drink and chatter, Zeus withdraws to a private chamber and puts on his robe.*

## SCENE SIX

*Dawn. Agamemnon's tent. As Agamemnon sleeps, Zeus steals into the room, kneels beside him and whispers at length into his ear. Before departing he examines Agamemnon's battle-plan on the table and helps himself to some fruit from the fruit bowl.*

AGAMEMNON (*stirring*)
  Odysseus. ODYSSEUS!

*Enter Odysseus*

ODYSSEUS (*rubbing his eyes*)
  It's very early.

AGAMEMNON
  It's time.

ODYSSEUS
  The cooks haven't even lit the fires.

AGAMEMNON
  Not breakfast. War.

ODYSSEUS
  This is very sudden.

AGAMEMNON
  The divine voice came to me in a dream.

ODYSSEUS
  Not a fever? The air was queasy last night, heavy in the lungs.

AGAMEMNON
  Almighty Zeus acknowledges us. I saw him, standing before me, the light cascading from his robes, a physical form.

ODYSSEUS
    Go on.

AGAMEMNON
    Troy with its high walls and broad streets is ready to
    fall. He said, 'Agamemnon, offspring of clever Atreus
    the horse-trainer, assemble your long-haired Greeks on
    the shore and prepare for battle.' Fetch me my tunic.

ODYSSEUS (*helping Agamemnon dress*)
    Why now, after ten years. Did he say?

AGAMEMNON
    You're asking, did I cross-examine the supreme being?

ODYSSEUS
    What were his reasons?

AGAMEMNON
    He listened to the pleas of his wife, Hera, and so did
    every god on Olympus. (*Regarding the tunic Odysseus
    has brought for him.*) Not this – the purple one. And
    now they speak with one voice.

ODYSSEUS
    It's decided then.

AGAMEMNON
    We'll ride the wave of Fate. And my cloak. Please. This
    might be over by the setting sun.

ODYSSEUS
    Troy reduced to rubble and ash.

AGAMEMNON
    Cinders where there were lavish throne rooms. Statues
    toppled.

ODYSSEUS

The men of Greece back in their homelands in a week.

AGAMEMNON

Boats low in the water with treasure and reward.

ODYSSEUS

Victory's smile smeared all over their faces. Your
brother's wife, returned to her own palace and kingdom.
Back in her own bed.

AGAMEMNON

Tell every commander to assemble his captains, every
captain to convene his officers and lieutenants, spread
the word right down to the last spear-carrier and cabin
boy and pot-washer – we'll go at them with everything
we've got.

ODYSSEUS

One last decisive push.

AGAMEMNON

Make it known.

*As those long-necked, ramshackle birds –*
*geese, swans, storks, cranes –*
*flock in water meadows off to the east,*
*then at some unknown signal*
*rise as one in a great cackle,*
*all wings and legs and pointed bills,*
*then screech and circle, till the air dazzles*
*and the earth rattles,*
*and men stand watching, cold and darkened*
*by sudden shadow . . .*

ODYSSEUS

*. . . so Greek warriors*
*will surge from the tents*

*and spill from the huts*
*and pour from their black ships,*
*and Troy's thick walls will tremble and flinch*
*with the drum and thunder*
*of marching men and horses' hooves.*
*And along the Scamander's grassy banks,*
*an army will muster,*
*like the petals and leaves of early summer,*
*more glittering, though, and greater in number.*

ZEUS
*As a forest fire*
*makes a burning beacon*
*of a whole mountain,*
*and the blaze can be seen from distant kingdoms . . .*

*. . . so forces will gather,*
*morning sunlight glowing like flames*
*on the bronze spears and the bronze shields*
*and shining armour, a brightness reaching*
*right into the heavens.*

THETIS
*As delirious flies*
*swarm in spring*
*when creamy milk oozes and drips*
*from the tits of sheep . . .*

ACHILLES
*. . . so Greeks are drawn forward,*
*thirsty for blood,*
*all too eager.*

ATHENE
*As practised stockmen*
*sort and sift*
*when goats and sheep*
*have flowed together,*

HERA

> . . . *so captains and chiefs*
> *will shepherd and herd,*
> *telling clans from tribes,*
> *men from boys;*
> *some to brawl at the front,*
> *some to push from behind*
> *some to hold the line.*
> *And there in the middle*
> *Lord Agamemnon,*
> *king among people,*
> *bull among cattle.*

AGAMEMNON (*to Odysseus*)

It's true I haven't always been Zeus' favourite. Look how he made me bicker with Achilles over the girl – I admit I raised my voice – then we both lost out. But it's of no consequence now. My silver sword, please, and the sceptre which empowers me – hold it with care.

ODYSSEUS

You should address the men once you're ready.

AGAMEMNON

But he favours me now. The dream was indisputable. No doubting it was meant for my ears, or that it came directly from his lips.

ODYSSEUS (*passing him a wooden crate*)

Stand on this.

*Agamemnon climbs on to the crate, then addresses the Greek forces.*

AGAMEMNON

The wind is behind us, the weather is with us, and so are the gods. But first, a calculation. Roughly speaking our numbers are equal on either side, and today we must

[31]

fight man for man. But what a ragtag outfit of half-breeds and strays they are, outcasts and misfits from every tinpot country this side of the Aegean. In fact if we ourselves fell into groups of ten, with one actual Trojan assigned to each company to pour our wine, I believe most of us would go thirsty. There's no heart there, and where there's no heart, *there's no hope.*

ODYSSEUS

That's good. More like that.

AGAMEMNON

Men of Greece, make your spears keen, your shields solid, your horses strong, your wagons sturdy and fast. By the time night comes those blades will be blunted, shields dinted and dulled, the muzzles of your mares and stallions white with foam. Your own arms and hands will be numb with the weight of weapons and the shock of metal clashing with metal, echoing into the bone. Cowards who hide by the boats or slink from battle will be thrown to the dogs and crows. But Zeus has spoken, let Troy reel and shake when the might of Greece comes hammering at its gates. Let our victory begin.

*The men roar their approval.*

First, a sacrifice to the Almighty, the father of the skies.

*During the following scene, Agamemnon and Odysseus prepare their offering to Zeus, making their prayers and scattering grain over the sacrificial bull.*

**Zeus**

I couldn't begin to count the number of men assembled on this shoreline, massing here ready to fight. Ordinary men who ten years ago said goodbye to their families, put aside their ploughs and their fishing nets and took up weapons of war instead. Men of the mainland and men of the islands, men from cities and villages, mountains and coastlines, men from many kingdoms and counties and states, all fighting here under the flag of Greece, under Agamemnon's command.

Men of Boeotia, in fifty ships.

Men of Orchomenus, a contingent of thirty ships.

Forty dark ships full of men from Phocis.

Forty black ships full of men from Locis.

Long-haired, fleet-footed men of Euboea – forty ships.

Men of Athens – fifty black ships.

Twelve ships from Salamis.

Eighty ships from Argus.

Men from Mycenae, a hundred ships, Lord Agamemnon's very own.

The contingent from Lacedaemon, some sixty ships.

The contingent from Pylos, numbering ninety ships.

The sixty dark ships of Arcadia.

Four captains from Elis each with ten ships at their command.

Men of Dulichium, a fleet of some forty ships.

Of Aetolia, forty ships.

Of Crete, eighty ships.

Countless men of Rhodes.

Of Syme, three ships.

Thirty ships from Cos.

Forty black ships from Phylace whose leader was the
first man to leap ashore a decade ago, and the first of the
Greeks to die.

Men of Pherae.

Philoctetes' men, in seven ships, each with fifty oarsmen,
skilled in shooting with the bow.

Of Tricce, thirty ships.

Of Ormenion, forty ships.

Of Argissa and Gyrtone, of Orthe and Helone, and of
Oloosson, forty ships.

Twenty-two black ships from Cyphus, near where the
river of death flows.

And the Magnetes of Mount Pelion where the leaves
quiver on the boughs – forty black ships.

Let it be recorded that these are the men who make up
the Greek force.

*Odysseus holds back the head of the bull and Agamemnon
slits its throat.*

AGAMEMNON
Almighty Zeus, we thank you, and we beseech you.
Hear our prayers.

## SCENE SEVEN

*Olympus. Zeus is consulting a book. Athene is embroidering.*
*Hera is restless.*

HERA (*looking to earth*)
    The glint of a fire. The unmistakable odour of singed hair
    and roasting flesh. The distant murmur of supplication.
    It can only be for your eyes, Zeus, your nose, your ears.

ZEUS
    Busy, thank you. Not to be disturbed.

*Hera leads Athene by the arm to a quiet place.*

HERA
    How can you sit there stitching while the Greeks march
    to their death?

ATHENE
    Patience.

HERA
    He acts as if we don't know. Thetis flutters her eyelashes
    at him, so he inflames Agamemnon's mind with a
    destructive dream, sends him wandering into a
    deathtrap.

ATHENE
    Keep your voice down.

HERA
    He won't hear. He's too busy being deaf, ignoring the
    prayers and pleas of the Greeks. How do I know it's
    a plot – did you ever know Zeus turn his back on a
    compliment before?

ATHENE
    He's watching. Admire my embroidery for a moment.

HERA (*under her breath*)

I haven't nursed and watched over that army for ten
years just to see them sent to slaughter, just so Achilles
can gloat at their downfall. What kind of turncoat is he?

ATHENE

Hera. Sometimes the scales can be tipped not by adding
more weight to one side, but by taking from the other.

HERA

Of course. I told you that. But what does it mean?

ATHENE

We can't stop the Greeks now, they're swarming like
bees. And I agree, Agamemnon's men are weakened by
disease and discomfort, no match for a well-fed army
fighting on home soil from behind an impregnable wall.
But what if the whole war came down to a straight fight
between two men, between a proven warrior on one
side, on our side, and on the other side let's say . . . a
more sensitive soul.

HERA

Why would anyone take such a risk?

ATHENE

Men can wake with strange ideas in their head, after a
dream.

HERA

You embroider beautifully, grey-eyed Athene. You work
such fine threads.

## SCENE EIGHT

*Achilles' tent. Achilles and Patroclus are swordfighting.*
*Eventually Achilles knocks Patroclus' weapon from his*
*hand and pins him to the ground, the point of his sword*
*against his throat. The two of them laugh, Achilles hauls*
*Patroclus to his feet and they clasp each other in friendship.*
*As Achilles turns, Patroclus kicks away his back leg and*
*trips him. Achilles chases Patroclus out of the tent.*

## SCENE NINE

*Troy. Outside the Scaean Gate, the imposing fortified main entrance to the walled city. Paris (blonde, wearing a leopardskin cape) walks forward, a sword at his side, a bow and quiver at his back, and a bronze spear in each hand.*

PARIS (*shouting into no-man's-land*)
I am one man, and I challenge one man. Let the whole war be settled by duel.

*There is no reply. He walks further forward.*

Single combat. Send out your best Greek, let him meet this Trojan face to face.

*No reply. Then, for a moment, a mighty Greek warrior stands before him, bathed in light, his armour glowing, light glinting from his splendid weapons. Walking cautiously backwards, Paris retreats to the gate and bangs at the door. Eventually it opens and Hector emerges.*

HECTOR
What? Am I seeing things?

PARIS
I lost my courage.

HECTOR
Get back out there.

PARIS
I don't have the nerve.

HECTOR
I said get back out there before the other men see you dithering and wilting.

PARIS

Give me a moment.

HECTOR

Paris. My brother. The gods' gift to women, with your pretty face and silver tongue. Maybe you *are* a woman!

PARIS

This again?

HECTOR

Better for me to have had a sweet-looking sister than a brother like you. That much I could have explained.

PARIS

A duel was my idea, wasn't it? That took courage. I didn't see you striding to the front or raising your arm.

HECTOR

No one was more surprised than me, and proud, when I heard those words coming from your mouth.

PARIS

One moment I was dozing, the next I was throwing down the gauntlet to the whole Greek army, the next I was sleepwalking into certain death.

HECTOR

I should have know you'd come scampering back like a mouse.

PARIS

He stood there, in front of me.

HECTOR

Such a great swordsman they say, but only in the bedchamber. Why were you even born – tell me? Better dead than the shameful creature that scratches here on the door, begging to come back in. Well, in some ways you've probably served your purpose, because those Greeks will have split their sides laughing by now.

PARIS

Get it all out of your system.

HECTOR

You were so brave when it came to stealing another man's wife, the lovely Helen, dragging her over the sea. Now half of Greece is camped on our doorstep, baying for blood. And do you know what troubles me most?

PARIS

What troubles you most, Hector?

HECTOR

That our own Trojans must be soft in the heart or soft in the head, because if they had any resolve they'd have stoned you to death a long time ago for the shit-storm you've brought down on them.

PARIS

Do you hear me denying it?

HECTOR

Your handsome face and clear skin and golden locks won't look so attractive when they're trampled in the ground, along with every other man in this city, and every child is skewered on a pike or lying sprawled and broken in a puddle of blood, thrown from the battlements, and every woman gang-raped and dragged off to Greece in leg-irons and chains. Every woman and child, including *my own*.

Pause.

I go too far.

PARIS

I know what I am in your eyes. How I compare.

HECTOR

Give me the weapons. I'll take your place.

PARIS

Like you, I am what I am, Hector. Aphrodite gave me
my talents and gifts, and most of my life I've been
thankful for them.

HECTOR

There are plenty that envy you.

PARIS

Even you on occasions.

HECTOR

On occasions.

PARIS

But you shouldn't fight this duel.

HECTOR

I shouldn't?

PARIS

Let the chance of glory fall to another man.

HECTOR

Noble and valiant. Spoken like a Trojan and a true
brother. I'll be with you in spirit, Paris, every throw of
the spear, every slash of the sword.

PARIS

No, you misunderstand me . . .

HECTOR (*emphatically*)

There's *no* misunderstanding, either on my part or
yours. The Greeks and the Trojans can watch from the

trees and balconies. To the winner, all the gold they can
carry, and Helen's hand. Then both sides must swear a
pact of friendship and peace, and the Greeks can return
to their country of horses and tall grass, and we can
open the gates of our walled city whenever we like,
without fearing the warrior's spear or the assassin's
knife.

PARIS
But I can't win this fight. It's as good as a surrender.
A sacrifice.

HECTOR
History loves the man who takes his place at the
appointed hour. (*Shouting.*) Trojans, Greeks: if you hear
me, lay down your arms. The man who made enemies
of our two great nations will meet your own champion
on the flat meadow of the river Scamander, and let the
outcome of their fight be the outcome of this war. Then
let this ten-year feud be over. Trojans, do you hear my
command?

*The Trojans (off) roar their acknowledgement.*

HECTOR
Men of Greece, do I have your word?

*The Greeks (off) roar the same.*

PARIS (*resigned, picking up his weapons*)
Hector, tell our father . . .

HECTOR
I've always believed I'll die before you. I still believe it.
You have a charmed life.

*Paris walks forward into no-man's-land. Hector watches him
go, then goes back into the walled city and bars the gate.*

## SCENE TEN

*A parapet above the Scaean Gate. To a fanfare of trumpets King Priam appears, ready to witness the duel.*

*Hera and Athene are watching from above.*

HERA

What is he thinking?

ATHENE

He sees in his son something of his younger self. Bow and arrow on his back, sword at his hip, spear in each fist. A heavy shield strapped to his forearm. He thinks, 'That could be me walking down to the riverbank, taking those steps. But I'm a spectator now, too old to fight.'

HERA

Or maybe he's wishing his other son were fighting for Troy instead, the man-slaying Hector.

ATHENE

Hector would stand a better chance, true, but if he died it would leave a bigger hole in Priam's heart.

HERA

Ah, poor Priam. One spectator among thousands. Look at them all. An hour ago two armies were ready to collide, and to go on slaughtering until the last man alive raised his fist in victory. Now the whole valley's an amphitheatre and they're the audience, leaning on their weapons, shouting and jeering. Suddenly it's a game. A game of our making.

ATHENE

A game of *my* making.

HERA

A game we can't lose.

ATHENE

Is your husband an onlooker too?

HERA

I visited his bedroom earlier. He sleeps now.

*Hera and Athene fade from view. Priam stands patiently on the parapet, eyes towards the battlefield.*

PRIAM

Come forward, child. No need to stand in the shadows. You're out of range. Out of view.

*Wearing a white veil on her face, Helen comes to stand at Priam's side.*

PRIAM

They say you were born from an egg.

That your father was a swan, hence the whiteness, the pale skin.

*Pause.*

Would you prefer to sit?

HELEN

You've always shown courtesy.

PRIAM

You're our guest.

HELEN

They have a new song about me, your people.

PRIAM

We have songs about everyone. We're a song-singing nation.

HELEN

*Helen of Greece, Helen of Troy,*
*married a man then married a boy,*
*the boy took her home, the man chased after,*
*all the way from stony Sparta . . .*

PRIAM

It has certain merits. A catchy rhythm.

HELEN

*Oh is it the eyes and is it the lips . . .*

PRIAM

You don't have to go on . . .

HELEN

*Or is it the thighs and is it the hips*
*That launched a thousand angry ships*
*And fired a million fiery darts*
*That pierced a hundred thousand hearts*
*And left a hundred thousand dead*
*And dyed the blue Aegean red*
*from Troy to Sparta,*
*all the way over the wind-blown water.*

PRIAM

*Helen of Joy, Helen of Slaughter.*

HELEN

I hadn't heard that last line.

PRIAM

The local poets have never been able to resist a convenient rhyme, no matter how crude.

*Pause.*

HELEN
How will this end?

PRIAM
The gods will decide. Or would that now be considered an old-fashioned thought?

HELEN
Non-believers never seem to fare any better.

PRIAM
Are you following today's developments? You're a foreigner here – can you read the situation?

HELEN
I recognise that lone figure.

PRIAM
Of course. My loving son, your loving husband.

HELEN
I am Paris' wife only under Trojan law.

PRIAM
So point out some of those other characters to me. You must know them, being one of them.

HELEN
Sir, I'm a harlot in the eyes of most people. It's a life of tears.

PRIAM
The seated one. Who's that?

HELEN
Lord Agamemnon, son of Atreus. A king among men.

PRIAM

He has a leader's profile. I visited his country once.

HELEN

Odysseus.

PRIAM

Famous Odysseus, with the sharp mind and the quick
tongue.

HELEN

But no Patroclus. No Achilles.

PRIAM

And the other man standing, fearless-looking, armed to
the teeth. The one who walks out to do battle with my
son. Do you recognise him?

HELEN

I do.

PRIAM

A name?

HELEN

Menelaus. My . . .

PRIAM

Your husband. I know. So your husband will slay your
husband, then you'll be carried off in your husband's
arms. Tell me, who else but the immortals could have
plotted that?

*Priam lifts Helen's veil and studies her face.*

PRIAM

You have the looks of a goddess – in weaker moments
I see you as my son does. But a curse to us all the same.

The life of all my people might bleed away into the sand because of this face.

*He looks at her for a while longer then lets the veil drop.*

Have someone bring me the news. I don't trust these old eyes.

*Exit Priam leaving Helen looking out across the battlefield.*

## SCENE ELEVEN

*No-man's-land.*

**Zeus**

We'd been expecting resolution here today, a killer blow
to bring this great war to an end, but instead . . .
confusion reigns. The ground was measured out and lots
were drawn from a bronze helmet to determine who
would throw first. And both armies roared their praises
to Zeus in heaven, and the noise of so many men
clamouring with one voice was unearthly. Paris, in
shining armour, stepped on to the field and took his
place, and Menelaus, dressed no less magnificently, did
likewise, and their followers watched, open-mouthed, in
dumb silence. Paris threw first, his long spear slicing the
air but striking the other man's shield and bouncing
away. Then Menelaus took aim, hurled his heavy spear,
and it ripped through Paris' shield, pierced his breastplate
and bit into his flesh. Drawing his sword, Menelaus fell
on Paris and brought down the full weight of his silver
blade on his enemy's helmet, but the sword shattered
into fragments, into dust. Cursing Zeus for his bad luck,
Menelaus grabbed Paris by the plume of his helmet and
dragged him off in the direction of the Greek troops till
Paris was purple in the face, with the leather strap under
his chin cutting into his neck, closing his windpipe, his
eyes popping out like two white eggs. But just when it
looked as if Menelaus might rip Paris' head from his
neck or choke him to death, an unworldly mist closed in
around them, ghostly, thicker than smoke, clammy to
the skin. A mist from nowhere that rose up then melted
away, and when it cleared, Menelaus stood with the
bronze helmet of Paris in his hand, but Paris nowhere
to be seen.

No fog remains, but mystery shrouds this valley.

Uncertainty hangs in the air.

Confusion reigns.

## SCENE TWELVE

*Priam's quarters inside the city. Priam is in prayer. Enter
Hector.*

HECTOR
Father.

PRIAM
Hector. Lethal Hector. If only *you* had raised your fist at
the best of the Greeks today. Then we might still have a
city to call our own. And you would still have a brother.
And I would still have Paris as a son.

HECTOR
You grieve too early.

PRIAM
You quibble over my timing? Should I wait until his
body is laid in front of me, bloodless and ashen? Or do
they carry him home in pieces, his hand chopped from
his wrist, his pretty head slashed from his neck?

HECTOR
His hands, his slender fingers, his teeth, his eyes, his
smooth forearms, his lovely curls, his winning smile . . .

PRIAM
Stop.

HECTOR
All still connected, all in working order and joined to the
same man.

PRIAM
Victorious?

HECTOR

Not the word most people are using. Try 'escaped', or 'disappeared'. Try 'vanished into thin air'.

PRIAM

Into nowhere?

HECTOR

Into a sudden mist.

PRIAM

Mist? In this season, at this time of day? Only the hand of an immortal could conjure up such a cloud. The pendulum swings, the gods are on our side.

HECTOR

Paris stole Helen and they wanted vengeance. Then he cheats them out of a fair fight, and now they want justice as well. Don't you see, if the Greeks had lost heart, the gods have now given them all the resolve they need.

PRIAM

An hour ago we were dead and buried. Now we're alive – that's my reading of this. Act on it I say.

HECTOR

The fighters are bewildered. Even embarrassed.

PRIAM

Start with the women. Keep them busy – don't give them a chance to tempt the men into their empty arms. Have them meet at the temple of Athene and make a sacrifice to her.

HECTOR

Athene dotes on the Greeks, everyone knows as much.

PRIAM

Then who better to praise? Lay the costliest robe in the
kingdom at the foot of her shrine. Slay a dozen year-old
heifers whose flesh has never been bruised or strained –
spill their tripes and inner organs in her name, pray for
pity, beg for the sake of the wives and children. Then
bring the army to their battle stations, and let the true
conflict begin.

HECTOR

You reload my heart with courage, Father.

PRIAM

Your heart beats with my blood. My pride and my love
for you are the same thing. Let's drink a glass of sweet
wine together. Wine is the great comforter of the
exhausted man.

HECTOR

I'm no longer exhausted, I'm revived. And I'll need a
clear head and a keen eye to drive a spear though
Agamemnon's throat.

PRIAM

My true son.

HECTOR

So, before the tide turns.

PRIAM

Before the gods change their minds. Go.

## SCENE THIRTEEN

*Helen's chamber. Inside, a bed is fully draped with curtains and nets.*

HECTOR (*from outside, entering the room*)
   Join the other women at the temple of Athene. Helen, answer me. HELEN!

HELEN (*emerging from inside the bed*)
   This room is private. What gives you the right?

HECTOR
   It's Trojan soil. I'm the king's son. Make the connection.

HELEN
   What happened to courtesy?

HECTOR
   War – that's what happened. Or isn't that a good enough reason to drag a woman from her beauty sleep? Go to the temple, now.

HELEN
   To be what? The Trojan wife praying for the death of Greeks, or a Greek slut praying for the destruction of Troy?

HECTOR
   That's a question only you can answer.

HELEN
   I've asked it every day for ten years.

HECTOR
   You're the woman Paris chose, and Paris is the brother the gods saddled me with, and for as long as that's the case I'll do my duty by you and my duty by him,

wherever he trembles and hides. So go to the temple, it's the safest place.

HELEN

Admirable qualities. Enough to make him blush.

HECTOR

Blood rushing to Paris's cool cheeks – wouldn't that spoil his looks?

HELEN

Perhaps it would – see for yourself.

*Helen pulls back the net on the bed. Paris is lying inside.*

PARIS

Before you explode . . .

HECTOR

So this is where you crawled to.

PARIS

A goddess led me here. I couldn't resist.

HECTOR

You sicken me, Paris. Men are teetering at the grave's edge because of your roving eye, and instead of standing shoulder to shoulder on the front line you lie here in this nest of perfume, between this woman's legs.

PARIS

Your taunts and your jibes are well aimed. Do you hear me arguing back? But leave Helen out of it – just now she was urging me to return to the fight, handing me my shining armour and my sharp arrows.

HECTOR

Instead of single combat you should have challenged the best of the Greeks at seduction or pillow talk – that way you'd have won hands down, all the practice you've had, and with one of their own!

PARIS (*jumping up*)
How dare you?

HELEN
Let him say what he wants. I know what I am. I should have been blown from the mountains or swept into the sea the day I was born. Some day Paris will pay for all the chaos he's caused, I'm certain of it.

HECTOR
Pure Greek. Loyal to no one.

HELEN
I respect you, Hector. And somewhere deep down I believe you respect me too . . .

HECTOR
That would be a very deep place indeed, somewhere on the ocean floor.

PARIS
Where sunken treasure lies.

HELEN
But you dishonour yourself today, storming in here to demean your brother and humiliate me. Putting righteousness before responsibility.

HECTOR
What nonsense is this?

HELEN
The Greeks will be battering at the gates any moment, but what of your own wife, Hector? Where is she? And your baby son?

HECTOR
Andromache – she's safe. With the other women.

HELEN
Not if I know her. She'll be looking for you, Hector, but
where are you? You're here instead, because it's easier
to bark out abuse at others than comfort your own.

HECTOR
What do you know about family?

HELEN
Look at the pair of you. Two brothers. One a lover, one
a warrior. Both deserters.

*A battle horn sounds in the distance. Hector pauses, then
turns and runs from the room.*

## SCENE FOURTEEN

*Achilles and Patroclus are playing a board game. The battle
horn is heard. They continue the game until the horn is
sounded again. Achilles stands and kicks the game into the
air, sending the board and counters flying across the floor.
As Achilles stares out across the battlefield in silent fury,
Patroclus joins him and puts a consoling arm around his
shoulder.*

## SCENE FIFTEEN

*Hector emerges, dressed in his finest armour, and is presented with his weapons. Above him on the parapet over the Scaean Gate, his wife Andromache appears with their young son Astyanax at her side.*

*Zeus catalogues the Trojan contingent as they prepare for battle.*

**Zeus**
Just outside the solid walls of Troy there's a large mound, a vantage point known as Thorn Hill. That's where the Trojans gather, not one people but allies and armies from many lands.

Battle-hardened Dardanians.

Men of Zelia, who drink from the dark waters of Aisepos.

Men of Adrestia and Apaisos, rulers over Pityeia and steep-sided Tereia.

HECTOR
Warriors. Comrades.

ANDROMACHE (*softly*)
Hector.

HECTOR
Fellow Trojans, brothers in arms . . .

ANDROMACHE
Hector.

HECTOR (*turning to find her*)
Andromache? But it's not safe here.

*Hector scales part way up the wall, to within touching distance of Andromache.*

**Zeus**
Horsemen of Perkote, Praktios, Sestos, Abydos and Arisbe.

Spear-throwers of lush Larisa.

ANDROMACHE (*drawing back a little*)
Save a speech for your men, Hector, but hear mine. Look at yourself, a man possessed, gripped by death. What pity have you for your infant son and faithful wife, by tomorrow your bereaved widow and bastard child?

**Zeus**
Thracians from the banks of the swift-running Hellespont.

The fearful Cicones.

Paionians of Amydon who drink from the sweet waters of the Axios.

ANDROMACHE
Go, rally your men by the Hill of Thorns, give your orders, your stirring war cries and historic words, but not your life. Because that would kill me, Hector. It would kill me. And you have no right.

HECTOR
You know me, Andromache. My place is the front line.

**Zeus**
Muleteers of Enetoi and all the lands they hold power over.

The Halizones, silversmiths from distant Alybe.

HECTOR
If I shrink from this battle, how could I ever look another
Trojan in the eye, or show my face to the Trojan women
in their long flowing skirts? I see it coming, the fall of
this city, the death of my people, Troy a slag heap of ash
and bone. But it's the thought of you being dragged off
by some savage Greek that pains me the most.

*Zeus*
Mysians.

From far-away Askania, warmongering Phrygians.

HECTOR
A skivvy in a torn dress, carrying water from a well.
Greek women hissing and snarling when you walk past,
saying, 'How hilarious, the princess of Troy, now a
serving wench.'

*Zeus*
Maionians, from under the shoulders of Mount Tmolos.

Alien-tongued Carians, their leader in battle wearing gold
such as a Greek woman might wear, gilded in sunlight.

The Lycians of Lycia, who have looked into the
whirlpools of circling Xanthos.

HECTOR
I won't stand back and watch that happen.

ANDROMACHE
No, you'll be spared that sight, lying dead in battle.

*Hector climbs all the way on to the parapet to hold her in
his arms. He then reaches out for their son, Astyanax, who
hides behind his mother's skirt. Hector takes off his helmet
and places it on the floor.*

HECTOR
It's me, your father.

*Astyanax recognises his father and jumps into his arms.*

ASTYANAX
Daddy, my daddy.

*Hector and Andromache laugh at their son's reaction. Then beneath them, Paris strides out through the gate, dressed for war.*

**Zeus**
Fighters of Troy, loyal to noble Paris.

*Hector puts down his son and puts on his helmet.*

HECTOR (*to Andromache*)
Go to the temple with the other women.

ANDROMACHE
Please, Hector.

HECTOR
Go to the temple.

*Andromache turns and disappears from the parapet with Astyanax.*

**Zeus**
All under the rule of Hector, son of Priam of Troy, Hector of the shining brass helmet with its horse-tail plume, leader of men.

*Hector descends and stands shoulder to shoulder with his brother. Silence. The battle horn is blown. Further silence.*

HECTOR (*roaring*)
FORWARD!

*The Trojan forces surge on to the battlefield.*

## SCENE SIXTEEN

*A thundery evening. Agamemnon's tent. Agamemnon
agitated and pacing the room. Enter Odysseus, breathless.*

AGAMEMNON
Tell me. Quickly. QUICKLY.

ODYSSEUS
Let me rest first.

AGAMEMNON
Certainly, take all the time you need to fill your lungs
with air, while your countrymen might be breathing
their last breath.

*Pause.*

Apologies. I apologise. I await your report.

ODYSSEUS
Heavy losses. Hundreds slaughtered.

AGAMEMNON
But with some progress I suppose? What's our position
in the field?

ODYSSEUS
No progress. Backwards.

AGAMEMNON
Have they breached the ditch? We did excavate a ditch,
didn't we, as I instructed?

ODYSSEUS
The ditch holds, but not for much longer. Another day
and the Trojans will be pouring across it.

AGAMEMNON
   Are we so weak we simply watch them engineer a bridge
   right under our noses?

ODYSSEUS
   By tomorrow it won't be a ditch, more of a mass grave
   filled with the limp bodies of Greeks, and they'll simply
   stroll across it.

AGAMEMNON (*after reflecting*)
   You're not exaggerating, Odysseus, for effect, story-
   teller that you are?

ODYSSEUS
   Yes, I've embroidered here and there, but only to pretty
   things up. Believe me, the truth is uglier in every detail.

AGAMEMNON
   But it's quiet out there. Even the thunder of Zeus has
   stopped.

ODYSSEUS
   An overnight truce to cremate the dead. On our side at
   least. Those fires across the plain are probably Trojan
   feasts – they roast cattle and sheep and offer up thanks
   to the gods. While we put a torch to our friends.

*Agamemnon goes to the door of the tent and looks out
across the plain, then returns.*

AGAMEMNON
   We have till sunlight.

   Gather the men as calmly and as quietly as you can.
   Tell them to board the ships while we still have them.
   By dawn we'll be halfway home.

ODYSSEUS
   What are you saying?

AGAMEMNON

The gods have decided, turned their backs on us. Proud
as I am I won't send half the men of Greece to the Land
of the Dead for a lost cause. Let them see their wives
again, and their own shores. I'm no fool, and no monster.

ODYSSEUS

So a coward then?

AGAMEMNON

I forgive that remark. Your intentions are loyal. But you
won't bait me.

ODYSSEUS

Then go, but sail on your own. I haven't waded this
deep into battle and death just to creep away in the
darkness. We came here to conquer Troy – it's still there
on the hill – nothing's changed.

AGAMEMNON

Everything's changed – use your eyes, use that brilliant
mind of yours.

ODYSSEUS

It doesn't take a brilliant mind to work out a plan of
action, just an open mind to hear one.

AGAMEMNON

Well? I'm listening. I'm all ears.

ODYSSEUS

It's Achilles . . .

AGAMEMNON

No. NO. That's not a plan. That's just the name of some
pig-brained oaf who in case you hadn't noticed is sulking
like a spoilt brat in his tent over there. The mood he's in
he's more likely to fight for Priam than for me, so don't
call that a plan, it's a suicide pact.

ODYSSEUS

It's our best and only hope. I know it, you know it, and
so does every man on this beach.

AGAMEMNON

He's an ignorant knuckle-brain. Inhuman.

ODYSSEUS

Inhuman indeed. Not one of us.

AGAMEMNON

That's pure speculation. What proof is there?

ODYSSEUS

Have you seen him fight? Have you ever seen him injured,
or even so much as scratched? They say as a child he
was fed with lion's gizzards and the marrowbone of
bears.

AGAMEMNON

He'll eat anything – he's from the north.

ODYSSEUS

Spears bounce off him. I'm no slouch with a sword but I
wouldn't want to fight him, not even with one arm tied
behind his back and a sack over his head. Would you?

AGAMEMNON

He's flashy. An exhibitionist.

ODYSSEUS

He's a killing machine. That's why we brought him here.

AGAMEMNON

Oh yes, and with a tender heel, they say. Where his
mother held him when she dipped her darling boy in the
River Styx. Whoever heard of a hero with a susceptible

heel? Not to mention a tender heart. Him and that
drooling cousin of his, Patroclus.

ODYSSEUS
A whole army.

AGAMEMNON
Zeus alone knows what goes on in that tent of theirs
at night.

ODYSSEUS
A one-man genocide.

AGAMEMNON (*after a pause*)
What do you think it would take, exactly?

ODYSSEUS
What exactly have you got?

AGAMEMNON
I'll summon my assessors. Draw up a list of goods.

ODYSSEUS
But knowing Achilles, it'll take more than a few shiny
trinkets to win him round.

AGAMEMNON
I won't say sorry.

Not to his face.

## SCENE SEVENTEEN

*Olympus. Hera and Athene are dressing each other in armour.*

HERA

Agamemnon. Agamemnon.

ATHENE

Bending like corn in the wind. This way, that way . . .

HERA

It's a stormy night.

ATHENE

When will he start acting like a king? Never, I suppose, as long as we go rushing to his side.

HERA

But so handsome. Well, in his younger years.

ATHENE

Greek men are better looking than Trojans. It's a fact of life.

HERA

He'll find his strength in the end. It's just a question of lending encouragement and support until the right time.

ATHENE

Ensuring a fair fight.

HERA

That's how I see it.

ATHENE

Did you ever lie down with him?

HERA
Excuse me, I'm the wife of Zeus. And you're his daughter.

ATHENE
Did you wear a disguise? That's how the other gods do
it. As an owl or a wood-nymph.

HERA
It's frowned on, immortals and mortals mixing freely.
It leads to complications and rogue stock. Freaks, even.
Look at Achilles.

ATHENE
You have all the right answers, Hera.

HERA
And you ask all the wrong questions, Athene.

ATHENE
Shall we go? Assist the good-looking lions against the
hideous warthogs?

HERA
Ah, that's an easy one. The answer is yes.

*Enter Zeus, who has been standing to one side, overhearing
their conversation.*

ZEUS
The answer is *no*. Indefatigably, incontrovertibly and
indisputably NO. Am I heard?

ATHENE
Yes, Father.

ZEUS (*to Hera*)
Am I *heard*?

HERA

As far as the edge of Asia I shouldn't wonder, and all the
way to the icy poles.

ZEUS

There will be no more interfering on either side. I held
up the scales of war and the balance tipped in favour
of Troy. That is the judgement of Fate.

HERA

Thetis touched your hand and stroked your ego – that's
when the balance tipped.

ZEUS

You push me too far, Hera. All of you – don't dare to
contradict my word. I'll seize the next god who steps out
of line and hurl them into the shadows, into the yawning
abyss beyond the edge of the world, below Hades even,
where only worms crawl and serpents hiss, into the
everlasting dark.

HERA

What about the poor women of Greece, whose interest
we have at heart? You play with human lives yourself –
we're just following your example.

ZEUS

Try me. Tie a rope to my arm and take the other end
yourselves. Pull as hard as you like – you'll never shift
me an inch. But one yank the other way and I'll drag
you all into the heavens, and the land and the oceans
with you, and leave you dangling from a dim and distant
star for ever more. That's what power I wield on
Olympus. That's why my word is law.

ATHENE

We understand. Don't we, Hera?

HERA
   Perfectly.

ZEUS
   Let the battle for Troy run its course. The more we leave
   alone the sooner it will be over, it's dragged on long
   enough.

   Now, I have business on Mount Ida. Fetch me my gold
   cloak and gold whip, and saddle me my two horses with
   the flowing gold manes and hooves of bronze. And
   return *my* armour to the armoury. Then find another
   project to occupy your thoughts. Plant diamonds in the
   rocks, invent some new flowers. Bake a cake. But stay
   out of Troy, or I'll fling you both into Hell's jaws.

## SCENE EIGHTEEN

*Achilles' tent. Patroclus is polishing Achilles' armour. Odysseus is seated. Enter Achilles. He has been washing; his hair is wet and the upper half of his body is naked.*

ACHILLES
You look tired, Odysseus. And filthy.

ODYSSEUS
War's a filthy business.

ACHILLES
That depends who you fight with. Grubbiness tends to rub off.

ODYSSEUS
Hard to bury dead comrades without getting your hands dirty. But you look well, my friend. Healthy. Spotless.

ACHILLES
It's the glow that comes of a clean conscience.

ODYSSEUS
And rested. You seem very rested.

ACHILLES
It's the beach, the sea air.

ODYSSEUS
The sound of dying men isn't keeping you awake?

ACHILLES
I hear Hector occasionally, slicing through the soft underbelly of the Greeks, and the swish of arrows – gentle Paris picking off fleeing Greeks with his bow. But it's of no concern.

ODYSSEUS

Hector and Paris. Heroes of Troy, while Achilles bathed and snoozed.

PATROCLUS

I said we were busy. He said he'd wait.

ACHILLES

He's welcome. It's just banter. I have no quarrel with noble Odysseus.

ODYSSEUS

And Odysseus has no dispute with noble Achilles.

ACHILLES

Then let's drink to that.

ODYSSEUS

It's a peace offering I've come with.

ACHILLES

Of course. Why else would you be here – the local wine is putrid, the worst I've ever liberated.

ODYSSEUS

Lord Agamemnon seeks to repair relations. To that end, here's what he promises:

(*Reading.*) Seven tripods not blemished by fire.

Ten talents of pure gold.

Twenty shining cauldrons.

Twelve pure-bred horses, race winners, sure-footed, famed for their speed.

Seven women from Lesbos, skilled in arts and handicrafts, the most giving and seductive.

PATROCLUS
And Briseis?

*Briseis is led into the tent.*

ODYSSEUS
And Briseis. Who he wrongly took from you. With a pledge that he never once went to her bed, or called her to his.

All this he makes available now, without condition.

And further, should the gods allow that Troy falls, twenty Trojan women, yours to choose.

And seven well-appointed cities, all close to the sea, populated by wealthy merchants and landowners paying tributes and tax.

And on return to Greece, if you will do him the honour of becoming his son-in-law, the hand of one of his three daughters in marriage, to take back to your own kingdom, with a dowry to match her looks and status.

All of these things he offers you, Achilles.

And for my part let me say this. If not for Agamemnon, then for the Greek troops, who worship you like a god. Kill Hector, fill their eyes with glory. Become immortal.

PATROCLUS
Achilles?

ACHILLES
One thing is true – this can't continue. I recognise that fact. So go to Agamemnon and tell him everything I say, and tell him in public, so no one will be left in any doubt.

ODYSSEUS
  I'll do that.

ACHILLES
  My answer is no.

ODYSSEUS
  That's a very hasty response.

ACHILLES
  No to the man who can't tell cowards from lionhearts.
  No to the man who sits on his purple throne while men
  lay down their lives. No to the man who expects every
  civilian of Greece to follow him over the edge of the
  cliff. And no to the thief who calls himself a king: I won
  my prize and he took it from me. Brazenly robbed me of
  a woman I cared for. Robbed *me* – no one else. Well he
  can keep her, do what he wants with her, until his bed
  breaks or his fat heart bursts.

*Briseis turns and runs from the tent.*

  Mighty Agamemnon! Building his ditches and walls,
  driving in stakes, and all of it useless. Why? Because
  without Achilles fighting his battles and inspiring his
  men, he's no king at all, for all his crowns and robes,
  just a man in a dress. If the Greek ships are going up in
  flames then tell him to fetch a bucket of water from the
  sea. If his fighters are dying around him, tell him to pick
  up a shovel and dig their graves, and if he doesn't know
  one end of a shovel from the other, tell him to use his
  royal sceptre, or better still, his bare hands. Let him feel
  the grit of life under those milky fingernails.

  Don't goad me with Hector. Is that how crudely you
  bait the trap? I don't need to slay Hector to prove my
  point, only to pave the road to Agamemnon's victory, so
  Agamemnon the Magnificent can ride his chariot all the

way into the treasure houses of Troy and load his coffers
with rubies and amethysts and leopards' claws.

No. That's my answer, give it to him full in the face.
He's a shameless, self-serving dog who can't even look
me in the eye, and sends you to run his errand for him.
He'll get no help from me. He's cheated me once – never
again. If he thinks I'll be sweet-talked like some child,
Zeus must have scooped out his brains and put a dead
squid in his head. As for his gifts, I detest them, every
item, because they're soiled by his touch. Never. Is that
understood? Not if every gate were thrown wide, and
through every gate came two hundred horsemen
dragging chariots filled with furs and sharpened
weapons and precious stones. NO! Not if he gave me a
gift for every grain of sand or ear of corn the world over.

As for marrying into his family . . . I wouldn't mix my
blood with his if his three daughters had the last three
cunts on earth. I'd fuck a dead animal first – tell him
that, word for word.

Tomorrow I sail west. Three days and I'll be home, out
of this madness, and if the rest of the Greeks have any
sense they'll follow suit, because they'll never get beyond
those walls or through those wooden doors, not without
Achilles. Death – that's what waits for them here. Death
on a beach. Not even a burial stone. Wiped from history.
Wiped from memory. Erased.

See yourself out, noble Odysseus. I'm going to offer
prayers to Zeus for a safe passage. You should do the
same.

*Exit Achilles.*

ODYSSEUS (*to Patroclus, who is still polishing the armour*)
Is this who you are, Patroclus, Achilles' cleaner? What
else do you do for him?

[76]

PATROCLUS

Whatever I do, I do willingly.

ODYSSEUS

The famous armour. Not a mark on it. Some say it has
magical properties.

PATROCLUS

And some say it's the man who wears it.

ODYSSEUS

Is this why you came to Troy, to polish metal? So shiny
you can see your face in it – look, the face of a brass-
rubber, the face of a servant.

PATROCLUS

All I see now are your sticky fingerprints on the glaze.

ODYSSEUS

Tarnished. Like your reputation when you get home –
do you think you're going to be able to buff that up with
a bit of spit and a soft cloth?

PATROCLUS

I'll sleep at night.

ODYSSEUS

I doubt it. You wouldn't dare.

PATROCLUS

Is that a threat?

ODYSSEUS

You haven't thought this through at all, have you?
You're clueless.

PATROCLUS

Enlighten me.

**ODYSSEUS**
If the Greeks triumph at Troy . . .

**PATROCLUS**
Impossible . . .

**ODYSSEUS**
If we triumph without Achilles, he'll be forgotten. A
nonentity. The greatest war in our nation's history, and he
sat it out, brooding in his tent.

**PATROCLUS**
There'll be no triumph.

**ODYSSEUS**
The world's most famous warrior, and he fluffed his lines.

**PATROCLUS**
Without him they're doomed.

**ODYSSEUS**
And what does it look like, that doom? Death in battle
for some. But for two cowards who deserted the cause . . .
How will that feel, back in a country of orphans and
widows?

**PATROCLUS**
He's made up his mind – he wants a quiet life.

**ODYSSEUS**
There'll be no peace with a hundred thousand corpses
moaning in his ears, hiding behind his eyes.

Patroclus, he's stronger than you but he's younger, a
hothead. Besides, you promised his father you'd watch
over him, and you promised your own father the same.

**PATROCLUS**
Achilles is a grown man.

ODYSSEUS

    With the brain of a juvenile. This is the stuff of schoolboys
    – he's backed himself into a corner and he's no idea how
    to get out of it. He needs the one person he trusts and
    believes to step in and sort it out – but that person is too
    busy polishing, polishing, polishing, blinded by the light.

PATROCLUS

    Achilles is Achilles. If he says he won't do something it's
    written in iron – he won't.

ODYSSEUS

    Then do it for him. Take his place.

PATROCLUS

    What? That's meaningless. What an empty thing to say.
    How would I 'take his place'?

*Pause.*

ODYSSEUS

    Ride into battle flying his colours.

PATROCLUS

    Insane.

ODYSSEUS

    One lap of the field and everyone wins. The Greeks will
    think it's him and they'll surge forward, filled with
    spirit. Achilles won't have eaten his words. And you'll
    have honoured your bond with his father, with your
    father, with your country, with your countrymen and
    with your soul.

PATROCLUS

    Madness. Lunacy.

ODYSSEUS

    Genius.

PATROCLUS

It'll never work. Not in a million years.

ODYSSEUS

It's our only chance. And yours too.

PATROCLUS

But who's going to be fooled? We don't look anything like each other.

*Odysseus lifts the polished armour of Achilles on to Patroclus' body.*

ODYSSEUS

But you will do in this. And this. (*Placing the helmet on to his head.*) And with this. (*Handing him the famous shield.*) You're a warrior, Patroclus, not a houseboy. Now tell me that doesn't feel right?

*Patroclus puts on the armour and walks towards the battlefield.*

*End of Act One.*

# ACT TWO

SCENE ONE

*Present-day Troy.*

**Zeus**

The Greeks rally, the Greeks pull back. The Trojans
push forward, the Greeks rally again, the Trojans fall
back. A man on the ground coughing up his own lungs,
finished off with a club to the skull. A hungry spear
enjoys its fill of flesh. A hundred arrows bite like adders,
thirsty for blood. This man here, his first appearance in
the front ranks, lasts no more than a second, a bronze
spear passing clean through his chest. Horses on their
backs, wild legs stampeding the air. A ship on fire. A tent
on fire dances in flames then disappears. Hand-to-hand
fighting along the defensive ditch, fingers ripping through
nostrils and cheeks, a fist closing around a windpipe, a
man's thumbs pushed down into a man's eyes, into the
softness behind. A Trojan spear misses its mark but kills
another man anyway, takes away half of his head above
his ear, and Hades opens its doors. A chariot pulled by
a spooked horse ploughs a wide furrow through ranks
of standing men then comes to a stop, its wheels fouled
with the dead. A man's skin, that elephant hide in which
he's carried his whole being, just a soap bubble now
against heavy iron, sharpened wood, biting leather,
pointed bronze. Still walking forward, a Trojan in
flames, a human torch. A Greek, stripping armour from
a dead Trojan, stabbed in the neck by a Trojan, who's
stabbed in the ribs by a Greek, whose throat is slit by a
Trojan, who fights on with two arrows buried in his
thigh. A Greek warrior comes forward but trips on his
shield, exposing his bare midriff – a Trojan warrior
accepts the gift, drives and twists a long pike into his
spleen, has to stand on the man's shoulders to drag his
weapon out. A Greek foot soldier hooks a Trojan

charioteer in the roof of his mouth with his spear, levers him into the air like a fisherman landing a thrashing dolphin or shark. Spears hurled into a mass of humans, unable to miss. A man still kneels, headless, his head lopped off by Greek sword. A man runs forward into the flight of a spear, the brass point exposing his white teeth and the white of the jawbone, his eyes filling with red ink, blood bubbling out through his nose and lips, and death's dark cape spreads over him. The living steal in to salvage armour, to claim a helmet or shield as a prize, to drag their dead back to their own side. The Trojans rally, the Trojans pull back. The Greeks push forward, the Trojans rally again, the Greeks fall back.

## SCENE TWO

*Achilles' tent. Achilles is packing his personal effects into boxes and crates. Odysseus enters, hauling a rolled cloth on a cart.*

ACHILLES
You again. We've said all that needs to be said.

*No response.*

One visit, then another. Tongues might start to wag, Odysseus, might start saying you're not so loyal to Lord Agamemnon after all but a friend of Achilles. A sympathiser, no less.

*No response.*

(*Noticing the cart.*) A gift? Really? Pathetic. I gave him my answer, but he still thinks he can win me over with a goody bag, some little token of esteem. Is he deaf or just plain stupid? I said no to half his kingdom already, what can he possibly give me that comes wrapped in a dirty old sack? His own weight in Turkish delight, is it? His eldest daughter dipped in gold?

*Still no response. Achilles senses Odysseus' mood.*

What's in the sack, Odysseus? Something underhand? One of Agamemnon's dirty tricks?

ODYSSEUS
Not from Agamemnon.

ACHILLES
Then from yourself, Odysseus?

ODYSSEUS
Not from Odysseus. Not from any of the Greeks. From
Troy. From Hector.

*Pause.*

ACHILLES
An hour ago, I saw tears in the eyes of my black stallion.
Just the salt in the wind I thought. But when a horse
cries . . .

*Achilles unravels the cloth and discovers the bloodstained
body of Patroclus.*

ACHILLES (*uncomprehending*)
How?

ODYSSEUS
With great courage. Bravely.

He led from the front, wouldn't be held back. Three
times he stampeded into the Trojans, took out nine, then
twelve, then another nine, and even when his horse
buckled and the shaft of his spear splintered and his
sword shattered against a Trojan shield, he picked up
a rough stone and smashed the skull of one man, then
another, and murder was in his eyes.

But the gods weren't with him, Achilles. He took a blow
to the head, then got thrown to the floor. And as he tried
to withdraw, Hector, like a wolf smelling blood, sensing
a wounded beast, came directly for him, ignoring enemies
to left and right. While Patroclus lay on his back with
the sun in his eyes, Hector drove a bronze spear though
his stomach and into the earth.

And while he was pinned to the ground, his enemy said,
'So Achilles sends Patroclus to fight his fight and bring

back Hector's bloodstained shirt. Instead, I send
Patroclus to the underworld.'

And Patroclus, with his final breath, said, 'Have this
moment, claim me as your prize. But already the bird
of death hovers over you; you're as good as dead,
slaughtered by Achilles. I'll leave the gates of Hades
open, Hector, you'll be joining me soon.'

All afternoon we fought for his body and brought him
home, but Hector took the armour – your armour – and
wears it, glinting and gloating on the walls of Troy.

ACHILLES
Patroclus fought in my armour? He fought as me?

ODYSSEUS
He fought *for* you. On your behalf.

ACHILLES (*accusingly*)
Was there a Greek hand in this? Or a Greek mind?

ODYSSEUS
Look to yourself first, Achilles. Reach for the mirror
before the sword.

*Exit Odysseus.*

*Achilles begins to wail in grief. He pulls at his hair, claws
at his skin, rubs sand and soot into his head and face,
distraught, all the time returning to the body of Patroclus,
kissing his hands, beating his chest, beating his own chest,
tearing at his clothes, attacking and smashing furniture in
the tent, howling, sobbing, dissolving in tears.*

*Thetis enters, dripping in water, covered in weeds and
flowers of the sea.*

THETIS
Achilles, my son. Why this? Why this?

**ACHILLES**

Patroclus.

**THETIS**

Such sorrow, Achilles. It travelled all the way to the seabed where I dozed. No mother could sleep through that grief.

**ACHILLES**

Look at the body of Patroclus, who I loved as a brother, who I destroyed.

**THETIS**

Put your head on my shoulder.

**ACHILLES**

Soft and pale, armour ripped from his pure flesh like shell from a crab. *My* armour, now on his killer's back.

**THETIS**

Rest first, Achilles; think with a calm mind, not with a clenched fist.

**ACHILLES**

There'll be *no* rest, not from here to the world's edge, until Hector dies.

**THETIS**

But it's written in Fate's hand. Kill Hector and you'll die at Troy.

**ACHILLES**

Then bring me my death.

**THETIS**

You ask a mother to start building her son's funeral pyre?

**ACHILLES**

Or hear him wail in horror till the end of his days, all the way down to the ocean floor, into the deepest trench, into the booming caves of the ear, echoing for eternity.

[88]

*Pause.*

I let Patroclus die. So give me revenge, a glimpse of
glory, then I'll lie at his side. Fate, maybe, but it's the
fate I choose.

THETIS

Then you'll have the armour you need, straight from
heaven's furnace.

But come to me first. Let us be mother and child for the
last time.

*Thetis kneels with Achilles, takes him in her arms, comforts
and nurses him, nourishes him with the milk of a goddess.*

THETIS

*Lame Hephaestus, blacksmith to the gods,*
*fashion for my son a second skin*
*of solid bronze, a carapace.*

*With metals from the volcano's mouth,*
*welded by lightning,*
*hammered by thunderbolt.*

*With metals forged in the fires of the earth,*
*then tempered and cooled*
*in Poseidon's garden under the waves.*

*Bring body armour beaten and shaped*
*on the anvil-headed rhinoceros,*
*then buffed by sandstorm, polished by love.*

*And a helmet that shines like a distant star,*
*and an ash-tree spear,*
*and a sword drawn from the glacier's heart.*

*And a shield like the moon.*

## SCENE THREE

*Troy. Priam, Paris, Andromache and Helen are gathered in a room. Enter Hector from battle, carrying Achilles' armour.*

PRIAM

Quite magnificent!

ANDROMACHE

Are you hurt? Let me look at that cut to your arm.

PRIAM

We saw it all from the battlements. Heroic. Achilles skewered like a squealing pig, and right in front of his men. Hector, with that thrust of the spear you've pierced the Greeks right to the core, punctured their whole army. This is the turning point.

PARIS

A pity he didn't bring back the body – we could have put it on display. The locals would have liked that, especially the women.

PRIAM

But he brings back the famous armour. Put that on display, impress the men.

HELEN

Who did you kill, Hector?

PRIAM

He killed Achilles – you were standing next to me, when he delivered the fatal blow.

HELEN

I've seen Achilles fight. Who did you kill?

PRIAM

Not Achilles? Look at the breastplate, these shin guards –
what cannot speak cannot lie.

HECTOR

Patroclus.

PRIAM

Achilles. Look at the shining helmet.

HECTOR

Achilles on the outside. But inside, Patroclus.

HELEN

They were inseparable.

HECTOR

Well, they've gone their own ways now. Patroclus to
Hades, Achilles to his sickbed no doubt, nursing a
broken heart.

PARIS

Are you sure about that?

HECTOR

I knew who it was, as soon as he slithered down from
that horse, as soon as he squirmed on the ground. But
it's better this way. They say Achilles has a vulnerable
heel, but it's bullshit, a distraction. What he has is a soft
spot for a friend, and I've just sliced the tendons, and the
heartstrings, and the guts.

PARIS

No. You've woken a monster. Tell him, Helen.

HELEN

I've never seen them apart.

ANDROMACHE

And you'll never see them together again now. Get used to that.

PRIAM

Not Achilles? Patroclus?

PARIS

Unkillable Achilles, now drawn into battle, blind with anger, with a bloodlust to satisfy. This is where your muscle-flexing leads us, brother Hector.

HECTOR

I've just won the war!

PARIS

You've signed our death warrant. Tell him, Father.

ANDROMACHE

Paris is wrong. Isn't he, Hector?

PARIS

We should plan an escape. Leave a small force here to buy time, but head east. There's an old tunnel that leads to the ridge. We have horses, camels . . . if we left at sunset, under cover of night . . .

HECTOR

Someone get this mosquito out of my ear before I swat it dead.

ANDROMACHE

But if there's an escape route? At least the children could . . .

HECTOR

I have the magical armour of Achilles, don't I? How could I fail?

PARIS

A man just died in that armour – how magical can it be?

HECTOR

That man wasn't Hector. Have them reopen the gates.

PARIS

To let Hector out or the tide come flooding in?

HECTOR

All this time I've been blaming you, Paris, saying that
Troy might be decimated because of your philandering.
But I was mistaken – you're quite brilliant. Annihilate a
whole generation of Greeks and we don't just win the
war, we win power for fifty years, a hundred years, for
centuries. No more scanning the sea for raiding parties
and black ships, no more listening for rattling swords,
no more storm clouds gathering in the west. A chance to
wipe the enemy from the face of the earth, without even
having to set sail, because you brought them right to our
shore. So congratulate yourself, brother – you haven't
just stolen a man's wife, you've castrated his country.
Paris, the saviour of a civilisation, the maker of empire.

PARIS

He's deluded. Tell him, Father.

PRIAM

Patroclus, then. Not Achilles.

HECTOR

There'll be no surrender. No retreat. It's time to stride
into battle, not follow the heels of women and children
into the desert and live out our lives crawling from one
dried-up waterhole to the next.

We are Trojans.

Of Troy.

Or we are no one at all.

*Hector departs. The others exit, Helen escorted by Paris, followed by Andromache, leaving Priam on his own.*

PRIAM (*aimed at Zeus*)
What will you have me see before I die?

*Out of sight, Zeus listens to Priam's words.*

Hector butchered by Achilles? Will you have me see that?

Visit me in the underworld, almighty Zeus, and tell me what I did to deserve this.

## SCENE FOUR

*Agamemnon's tent. At the table Agamemnon sleeps in his chair. When he wakes, Achilles is standing before him, dressed in the new armour and equipped for battle.*

ACHILLES
You should find new guards. I could have opened you up like a fish.

AGAMEMNON
Do I need guards? Against a fellow Greek?

ACHILLES
I'm ready to kill.

To avenge Patroclus' death.

To take down every man who had a hand in it.

AGAMEMNON
But your sword points at your king.

*Pause.*

ACHILLES (*returning the sword to its sheath*)
Your men are blunt and slow. They need a spearhead. Wake them, tell them to fall in.

AGAMEMNON
You'll fight again? (*Calling.*) Odysseus! Odysseus!

ACHILLES
My Myrmidons will take the front line.

AGAMEMNON
You've seen sense, Achilles. Odysseus will arrange the recompense, the tripods, the gleaming cauldrons and

suchlike, have them all crated up and taken to your tent.
Odysseus! He sleeps like a bear in winter!

ACHILLES

We'll attack before nightfall.

AGAMEMNON

The other items: the Trojan women and so forth, my
offer of cities and estates, all those details can be
finalised at a later stage, my daughter et cetera, I'll have
documents drawn up, binding on both sides.

ACHILLES

Gifts or no gifts, all I want is Hector dead, and every
Trojan that stands between his throat and this blade.

AGAMEMNON

It's what we all want. We want the same thing!

ACHILLES

And anyone who loves Hector – family or friend – to be
broken and beaten, one at a time, so pain and torture
are passed along to the last man, woman or child.
Stripped out – right to the root.

AGAMEMNON

So our differences are behind us, yes? Odysseus! I agree
of course, what has all this rancour achieved? It's a
bitter medicine you've had to swallow, Achilles.

ACHILLES

From a poisoned cup, Agamemnon.

AGAMEMNON

It's a reasonable point you make, and something I've
been reflecting on these past days . . .

ACHILLES

I'm sick of the argument. Just get your men on their feet.

AGAMEMNON
  . . . and what I've concluded is this. It was Delusion, no
  less! No other explanation?

*Enter Odysseus.*

  Ah, Odysseus, I'm just clarifying my position with our
  noble comrade Achilles. Ready the army.

ODYSSEUS
  They need to eat.

AGAMEMNON
  Delusion, who never walks on the ground but flits about
  in the ether whispering idiot thoughts in the minds of
  men – Delusion made me take your prize.

ACHILLES (*to Odysseus*)
  Why aren't you rousing the troops?

ODYSSEUS
  They're ravenous. They can't fight on an empty belly.

AGAMEMNON
  Then Delusion with her blindfold, so even though
  Hector was running wild in the battlefield and Greeks
  were being mown down, I couldn't see, because all the
  time her hands covered my eyes.

ACHILLES
  I'm hungry myself, but only for bloodshed and the cries
  of dying Trojans.

ODYSSEUS
  You'll give them heart, no doubt about it, but that will
  only take them so far. They need the night to recover
  and refuel. Advise him, Agamemnon.

ACHILLES

Patroclus lies dead on a makeshift stretcher outside my
tent. A spear hole as big as a fist in his chest, flies
dancing around his eyes and lips, the soles of his feet
facing the dusk. That's all the appetite I need.

ODYSSEUS

There'll be more lying next to him if we go into battle
unfed.

AGAMEMNON (*decisively*)

Let him go. Go, Achilles, before your blood boils and
bursts out through your veins.

But let's agree this. Too many days have passed in
slaughter and misery because of the feud between us.
No more locking horns – this grievance ends. What we
do now we do as one force. As Greeks. For Greece.
Give me your word on that.

*They shake hands.*

When it grips the hilt of the sword, let the fist of Achilles
be joined by Agamemnon's hand.

*Achilles strides out to battle.*

Feed the men. Once they're battle-ready, follow that
hurricane.

## SCENE FIVE

*Achilles and Hector meet in no-man's-land. Achilles is*
*wearing the new battle armour and carrying the shield*
*given to him by Thetis. Hector is wearing Achilles' old*
*armour. A long gruelling fight takes place.*

HECTOR

Even if we circle a hundred times round these city walls
I won't back down, Achilles. But let's make a pact in
hearing of the gods. If I kill you, I'll honour your death
and hand your body back to the Greeks. Tell me you'll
do the same, that if I die, you'll release my body to Troy.

ACHILLES

The lion doesn't make deals with the cripple, or the wolf
with the lamb. I'll bury this sword in your blood, that's
my only promise. Now fight.

*Priam emerges on the parapet above the Scaean Gate,*
*unseen by the combatants, and witnesses the rest of the*
*struggle. The fight continues until Achilles overpowers*
*Hector and stands above him, the point of his sword over*
*his throat.*

What did you think, when you stripped the armour from
my dead friend, sacred metal which you now defile with
your own presence? That I'd crawl away, or die of grief
over there by the hollow ships? THIS IS ACHILLES.
Achilles, who'll bury Patroclus with all the honours on
earth, and leave you rotting in a ditch until the dogs and
buzzards have eaten you down to your filthy bowels.

HECTOR

I beg you, as a man, as a son. Let me be ransomed for
bronze and gold and cremated in Troy, give my body back
to my father – think what your own father would want.

ACHILLES

Don't dare whisper my father's name. If it wasn't for
the eyes of my own men looking on I'd slice you and eat
you raw. No one is going to stop me throwing your
hacked-off head to the dogs. And there'll be no ransom
because there'll be no body to give back, just a smear of
grease and patch of bloodstained earth. Take that with
you as your dying thought.

HECTOR

The gods will never forgive you for abusing another
man's corpse. You'll pay with your life.

ACHILLES

I'm ready to die. Eternal death for this one moment of
pure pleasure – it's a fair price.

*Achilles plunges his sword into Hector and lets out a roar
of anguished relief. He drags the body to the Scaean Gate.
Under Priam's eyes he mutilates Hector, stabbing the body
over and over, cutting the tendons at the back of the legs.
Then with a leather strap he drags Hector by the ankles
back towards the Greek camp.*

*Andromache comes on to the parapet.*

ANDROMACHE

How could you watch?

What now of me?

What of my child, our little lord?

Who wears Hector's brow.

Who'll go begging now from bowl to bowl.

Tugging at sleeves. Little fatherless soul.

His walls destroyed, his tower brought down.

*Pause.*

And what of my husband, my lost world?

No limbs to wash, no eyes to kiss and close.

No arms to fold, no hair to comb.

He was delicate, under that fierce voice.

Such lovely garments, so lovingly stitched.

I'll go to his wardrobe. Burn his clothes.

*Andromache leaves Priam on the parapet. He begins to weep.*

## SCENE SIX

*Present-day Troy.*

**Zeus**
> There's a bad smell around this place. Unburied bodies,
> fussed over by bluebottles, watched from a distance by
> scavenging eyes, drooling tongues. Old flesh in a warm
> climate, foul meat. Patroclus in limbo lying washed and
> pale. Hector in limbo, matted and gouged.
>
> And the stink of bitterness, anger's open wound,
> Achilles still raw with fury. No matter how many times
> he grinds a spear or twists a knife into Hector's corpse
> the pain won't stop. For days now he's dragged that
> carcass round the city walls, under Priam's eyes, right
> under his nose.
>
> And a scent drifts out of Troy. The smell of grief: stagnant,
> queasy, stale.
>
> And all those smells curdle and mix in the slow air: the
> sourness of hate, grief's mustiness, the sickly sweetness
> of human death. Gas. Enough to make the stomach
> retch, and the eyes water, and the heart bleed.

**Hera** (*off*)
> Supper's ready. Zeus! Zeus!

**Zeus**
> I'm not hungry.

**Hera** (*entering*)
> I killed a chicken.

**Zeus**
> We had chicken the other day.

**Hera**

That wasn't chicken.

**Zeus**

You said it was chicken.

**Hera**

No. You said it was small, for a chicken. I never said what it was.

**Zeus**

Oh. I see. But this is chicken, is it?

**Hera**

Yes, and it's going cold. And we need batteries for the radio.

**Zeus**

I'll be along shortly.

**Hera**

Talking to yourself, telling your stories again. They'll come and take you away one of these days.

**Zeus**

Let them try.

**Hera**

What will you do? Turn into a raging bull? You're not the person you used to be – don't fool yourself, Zeus.

**Zeus**

Two minutes. Just a few ends to tie up.

**Hera**

Two minutes. Then it's going in the dog.

## SCENE SEVEN

*Achilles drags the mangled and mutilated body of Hector into his tent, drinks from a wine cask, then slumps on his bed and falls asleep.*

*The ghost of Patroclus stands before him.*

PATROCLUS
    Are you asleep? Have you forgotten me?
    You loved me in life but leave me now to rot.
    Burn and bury me, friend. Until I'm buried
    the spirits won't open the House of the Dead;
    I stalk the wrong side of the river, staring
    across the rapids into its rooms and halls.

    A last chance, Achilles, give me your warm hand.
    Once I've passed through the curtain of flames
    you'll never see me or hear me again,
    we'll never touch, or walk on stony hillsides
    scheming and gossiping, hatching our wild plans.

    My fate from birth – to be killed at Troy
    under its sloping walls – and your fate too.
    So when you die, have them seal your bones
    in a golden casket, wrapped with mine, so in death
    we'll be joined like brothers, as we were as boys.
    Build a pyre; throw on a lock of your hair. Achilles . . .

*Achilles stands and moves forward to embrace Patroclus, but he has vanished into the air. Achilles reels in bewilderment and sorrow. He sits on the bed with head in hands. When he looks up, a robed and hooded figure has entered the tent.*

ACHILLES
    Another phantom? The spirits are restless tonight.

*The figure takes off his hood. It is Priam. Achilles picks up his sword.*

ACHILLES
You come here? Right to my door?

PRIAM
I'm alone. Unarmed.

ACHILLES
I could slice off your head. I've every right.

PRIAM
I'm an old man. There's not much more of my life you can take.

ACHILLES
Only the gods could have ushered you through the Greek encampment and into this tent. I'll assume they're listening in.

PRIAM
I come here not as a fighter, but as a father. Achilles, think of your own father . . .

ACHILLES
It's not for you to invoke the name of a man you don't know.

PRIAM
Peleus is his name. A man my age. Grey-haired like me I suppose, his back beginning to curve, deep furrows across his brow.

ACHILLES
He's dignified and strong.

PRIAM
That was a decade ago. Alone, vulnerable, wondering

when his boy will return home. But at least he still has
hope. I have none.

ACHILLES
Men die. How else to win a war?

PRIAM
No human should have to look on their child's corpse.
It goes against all that's right in this world.

Yet now, to beg for his body, I have to do what no father
on earth has done.

I go to my knees.

ACHILLES
Don't. Priam.

PRIAM
I go to my knees,

and lift to my lips

the hand of the man

who killed my son.

*Pause.*

ACHILLES
Was there a worthier king?

PRIAM
I offer a king's ransom. A wagon outside the city gates
strains under its load.

ACHILLES
Come and sit at my table. I offer you wine and food.

PRIAM

I won't. I haven't eaten since you drove that blade into
Hector's throat. Haven't slept, watching the rag doll
of his body hauled across stones and through sand.
I beg you, as a father to a son, let me carry him home.

ACHILLES

Go back the way you came, Priam.

Send the treasure. It can go to Patroclus' father – that
would seem right.

Then I'll return the wagon.

*Pause.*

With Hector's body on it.

Let him be washed and clothed first.

You'll have him by first light.

PRIAM

There is honour between men. Honour between Troy
and Greece.

ACHILLES

But expect no other favours. Once battle resumes, every
man on this beach will want to hold up the trophy of
Priam's heart in his fist.

PRIAM

Then it's you they'll battle with, Achilles. You got there
first.

## SCENE EIGHT

*Olympus. A council of the gods. Present are Athene, Hera, Thetis and Zeus.*

ATHENE
A great conflagration on each side.

HERA
More sacrifices, is it?

ATHENE
Huge bonfires. One inside Troy, one on the beach.

THETIS
A truce?

ZEUS
Cremations. Patroclus and Hector. Two funerals.

THETIS
But no fighting for days. It could mean peace.

HERA
There will be no peace until Troy falls and Agamemnon lifts Priam's crown to his head.

THETIS
But if a deal has been struck, why more slaughter and sorrow?

ATHENE
Thetis, this is what you wanted, isn't it? Glory for Achilles. Have you changed your mind?

HERA
She went wheedling around my husband to get a hero's sword back in her son's hand, even gave him his new armour, and now she's trying to save his neck.

ZEUS
Please, everyone. I have a thought to share.

HERA
She's two-faced.

THETIS
And you're so smitten with Agamemnon you're blind
to the suffering of everyone else in the world. For a
goddess, you have an inanimate heart.

HERA
Butterfly.

THETIS
Mercenary.

HERA
Hypocrite.

THETIS
Whore.

ZEUS
Enough.

ATHENE
But you're no better. Wasn't it you who guided Priam
to Achilles' tent? How else could he have crossed the
battlefield unscathed?

ZEUS
It tortured my senses, watching the old man weep.

HERA
And what of Patroclus' father when he gets news of his
son? Will you hear his lament?

**THETIS**

Or Achilles, if he's fated to die in battle. What of his father's tears?

**ZEUS**

You're right of course. I thought I was healing a wound. But to what end? Tomorrow they'll pick up their weapons again.

**HERA**

But if we all pushed from the same side, maybe the Trojans would surrender – then lives would be spared.

**THETIS**

Or if Achilles retired from battle, now he's killed Hector.

**ATHENE**

But then we'd be right back where we started from.

**ZEUS**

On Mount Ida I looked into the everlasting, into the eternal void, and it asked me this: 'Does Zeus own the world, or does the world own Zeus?'

**HERA**

You're the almighty. You own everything.

**ZEUS**

That was my first response. But what if there were no Trojans, no Greeks. What if they fought right down to the last life. No one to praise or flatter us.

Would we still exist?

**ATHENE**

Of course we'd exist. And our lives might be a whole lot easier.

**ZEUS**

Doing what? Presiding over a world of lilies and kittens.

The dandelion won't build temples in our honour. The elephant won't trumpet our names. What would we do – take pride in the beetle while it pushes its ball of dung up and down the dunes? Assist in the spinning of a spider's web?

HERA

Highly philosophical I'm sure, but what's your point?

ZEUS

We need believers, people of faith. If we sympathise – rule with a bleeding heart – then we favour the weak. And the weak are fickle, and disappointed, diseased. The weak are weak. Do we put our future in their shaking hands?

ATHENE

You're saying . . . let the powerful survive. Those of the strongest arm.

ZEUS

And the quickest hands, and the deadliest aim, and the sharpest mind. It might be tomorrow or it might take another ten years. But someone will triumph, either through muscle or brain . . .

THETIS

And they'll be worthy of our praise.

ZEUS

. . . and we of theirs.

Now, enough words have shuttled between us on this, I deem the meeting closed and the matter settled.

I'm so exhausted I could sleep for a month. See that I'm not disturbed.

## SCENE NINE

*Outside the walls of Troy. Some days have passed. Priam, Helen and Andromache, who is in mourning, are standing beneath a huge wooden horse.*

PRIAM

It seems more massive and intricate closer up than it did from the city walls.

HELEN

Was it made by men or by gods?

ANDROMACHE

Horses are soulful creatures. This radiates malevolence.

PRIAM

Look at the beach. Yesterday a city of prows and masts. Now golden sand again, just the odd broken oar and length of rope. And this horse.

ANDROMACHE

Ten years trying to suffocate Troy, then overnight they disappear. For what reason?

HELEN

Why have you thrown that question towards me?

ANDROMACHE

You're a Greek. You have a Greek mind.

PRIAM

I can't work out which is more puzzling. This horse, or the emptiness around it. Is this what victory looks like?

*Enter Paris, dragging a dirty and bruised young man, Sinon. His hands and feet are shackled and there is a rope around his neck.*

PRIAM
Who's this poor wretch?

PARIS
He was caught by farmers, hiding in the corn. He's a
Greek. Aren't you?

SINON
I am Sinon. A Greek.

PRIAM
From Agamemnon's army?

SINON
From Agamemnon's army. I am Sinon. A Greek.

ANDROMACHE
Haul him up. Let him hang from the horse.

PRIAM
Wait. Where are your people? What's the meaning of
this construction?

HELEN
The rope's too tight.

ANDROMACHE
Pull it tighter. Let him know how a stranglehold feels.

PARIS (*loosening the rope*)
Let's see if he can breathe a few words of truth first.

SINON
I am Sinon, a Greek.

PARIS
Yes, yes, we've established that.

SINON
The gods visited the camp.

The brightness was blinding. A golden array. They said we violated sacred earth, holy ground.

PRIAM

The gods recognise our land and people. I always believed so.

ANDROMACHE

It's a trick. They're born liars.

PRIAM

Why did they leave you?

SINON

I worked for Odysseus. Witnessed his rage, temper, abuse. Crimes of brutality against his own kind. To keep me from talking he said the gods had singled me out, to be sacrificed.

They shaved my head. Tied ribbons around my ankles and wrists. Put a blindfold over my eyes.

They stacked wood. Hoisted me up. Lit the fire. But the pile of timber tilted and spilt, threw me clear. So I bolted, couldn't see, tripped and fell again and again but ran and ran until the shouts of the Greeks and the sound of the sea fell away, and I smelt meadows and fields, and felt corn stalks brushing against my bare arms, and whiskers of corn on my face, and that's where I laid down, and curled up, and went to sleep.

PARIS

What makes you think you're safer with Trojans than you were with Greeks?

SINON

I always expected to die at Troy. But not burnt alive by my own captain. And as long as he thinks I'm alive he'll

never rest, wondering if I'll walk into Athens or Ithaca
one day, telling my tale.

PRIAM
Untie him.

ANDROMACHE
No.

PRIAM
But I still want him to explain the horse.

ANDROMACHE
Oh, he will. I'm sure he's got a story ready to tell.

PARIS
Well?

SINON
Zeus himself put his finger to Agamemnon's forehead.
Made him swear an oath to construct this gift for Troy,
a monument and an apology. But bombastic Agamemnon,
even though the Almighty had seared his fingerprint into
his brow, he ordered his Greeks to build it too high to
fit through the city gates.

PARIS
He disobeyed the god of gods?

SINON
So it would stay on the beach. To prove that the
seagoing empire of Greece laps at the shores of Troy.
To stand in the eyeline whenever Troy looks west. To
remind Troy how Greece sailed right to its doorstep and
took the life of its best prince. That was Agamemnon's
parting speech – I remember it word for word.

PRIAM

Have it measured, call for the royal carpenters and engineers. We're taking it in.

ANDROMACHE

No. Topple it into the sea. Set fire to it. Drive a spear though its belly.

PARIS

We'll build a plinth for it in the main square.

PRIAM

A lesson for generations to come. Of unconquerable Troy.

PARIS

To say that nobody enters this holy city, except by our decree.

PRIAM

What is ours is ours.

ANDROMACHE

Wait. Please. Helen, sing.

PARIS

A song of Troy! Yes. She has the voice of an angel.

ANDROMACHE

A song of Greece. Something sad and slow. Sung in the voice of a lonely woman.

PARIS

Isn't that a bit miserable, under the circumstances?

HELEN

She thinks there are Greek soldiers hiding inside, waiting to pounce. Isn't that right, Andromache?

ANDROMACHE

Like the Greek hiding inside Helen. That's why she
reads my mind.

HELEN

And that by singing a song of home I'll make them weep
for their land or their wives. Then we'll hear them, or
see their tears dripping through these beams and boards.
Yes?

PRIAM

So what if there are? What would it hold – five or six at
most? They'd be double prisoners – walled inside Troy's
stronghold and caged in a wooden horse.

But yes, have her sing if you must.

*Walking around the horse, Helen sings the sad 'Song of the
Lonely Wives' in Greek. Sinon begins to weep.*

*Silence.*

PRIAM

That would have melted the heart of an ox. If there are
men within this structure, they are either dead or carved
from marble.

PARIS (*speaking of Sinon*)
But this man sobbed, so the song hit the mark.

SINON

I left a young bride. I can barely picture her face.

PRIAM

Forget her. In return for your confession, I grant you
your freedom. Find a new wife in my city. You are
Sinon, of Troy.

SINON
I am Sinon. Of Troy.

PARIS
A Trojan. One of us.

PRIAM
All those who bear witness say 'Aye'.

*They all say 'Aye', Andromache reluctantly.*

PRIAM
Open the gates. Even if we have to take down the bridge and widen the arch, this horse is ours.

*The wooden horse is taken into Troy.*

## SCENE TEN

*Night. Inside the city. Alone in the main square Sinon*
*opens a hatch in the horse. Achilles, Odysseus and*
*Agamemnon climb out.*

AGAMEMNON

No sentries on duty?

SINON

They've all been stood down. What did you think of my
performance?

ODYSSEUS

Prizewinning. Remind us never to believe anything you
say.

SINON

I had a good teacher, Odysseus. But I thought there were
five of you.

AGAMEMNON

Two started weeping at Helen's song. Odysseus had to
slit their throats.

SINON

What about the blood?

ODYSSEUS

The Greek fighting helmet makes a useful bucket.

AGAMEMNON

Is the flare lit?

SINON

Blazing from the highest roof, and the fleet already back
on the beach. It never occurred to Priam that they were
only a mile off the coast.

ODYSSEUS

I'd worked out the lines of sight. Tenedos Island was the perfect hiding place. It could have been designed by the gods.

ACHILLES

So could Troy. It's spellbinding. Magnificent.

AGAMEMNON

Enough dreaming and enough talk. Count to a thousand – until the army have crossed the beach – then open the gates. They know what to do.

Every man to be killed. Every woman to be marked with a blade, then chained. No child to be spared – no matter how sweet or cute, we're not going to suckle a litter of snarling wolves.

Move with soft feet, the more we kill in their sleep the less risk to our own. Set fires and lock doors, let smoke and flames do the work.

Seek out the king's quarters. Hoist Priam's head on a stake.

Find Helen. Bring her to me.

Go. Desecrate.

## SCENE ELEVEN

*Priam's chamber. Priam is watching the destruction of his city. Screams, howls and crashes are coming from every direction. Fires rage all around. Andromache enters.*

ANDROMACHE
I saw the Greeks flood through the gates, a black tidal wave. Where were the guards? The screams of women – that was the only alarm.

Paris has secured the inner quarters with the royal guard. Archers have come to the turrets, and the first attack is repelled.

PRIAM
It's over.

ANDROMACHE
They say the north and the east gates are still closed. And the stockade is safe. And the bridge between the outer wall and the upper courtyard – no enemy could pass across it alive – it's a bottleneck.

PRIAM
Look down from this ledge. It's over. Where is your child?

ANDROMACHE
In the high temple with the women and maids.

PRIAM
Go to the tunnel while you can.

ANDROMACHE
Come with me.

PRIAM
No.

ANDROMACHE
If we have to flee then at least lead us forward, show us the way.

PRIAM
I won't do that.

ANDROMACHE
Then what, sit here till they burst through the door? They're swarming out there, thousands of them, all hunting for your head.

PRIAM
Ten years ago I saw them come. The black ships. Just a speck on the horizon. A pinprick. Now we're swallowed up in their dark gut.

Help me with this.

*Priam has unpacked a set of ancient and outmoded armour.*

ANDROMACHE
Priam, no.

PRIAM
I nearly threw it out years ago. Help me, it ties at the back.

ANDROMACHE
What are you doing? No one could fight in this, it's a museum piece.

PRIAM
And I'm an antique. Oh, a bit tight here and there but not a bad fit. And the helmet, please. A bit battered, but at least the plume's still bright and proud, not at all . . . what would you say . . . crestfallen.

ANDROMACHE
They'll hack you to pieces. You won't make it more than a few strides.

PRIAM
And the spear. And the sword.

ANDROMACHE
You can hardly lift it.

PRIAM
True, it seems to have gained weight over the years. But my hand still fits the hilt, as if I never let go.

ANDROMACHE
Priam, take us through the tunnel. Think of your grandchild, Hector's son.

PRIAM
It's over, Andromache. The House of Priam burns. If he lives, your boy, he'll be the prince of nothing, a scavenging rat on a mound of litter and bones. And I'll be a toothless old mouth to feed. So let his inheritance be memory: his father who died in glory defending Troy, and his father's father, who died the same way. Let him draw strength from that.

ANDROMACHE
You choose death in battle over a life of embarrassment. Just as Hector did. That was his weakness.

PRIAM
Go to the temple.

ANDROMACHE
You don't have to do this.

PRIAM
And then to the tunnel.

ANDROMACHE
    Priam.

PRIAM
    I'm needed at the gate.

*Priam walks into the battle. Andromache turns and runs.*

*The noise of fighting resonates through the city, and the room glows with the reflection of fire.*

*Enter Helen. She watches from the window, then kneels before a statue of Athene to pray. Enter Achilles, carrying Priam's helmet in his hand. Helen's back is turned to Achilles.*

ACHILLES
    Do you recognise this voice?

HELEN
    From a Greek mouth. Like an echo I thought had died out.

ACHILLES
    Is it a welcome noise?

HELEN
    These walls are a thousand years old but have never heard that language.

ACHILLES
    These walls will be cobblestones by morning. What you hear is an earthquake.

HELEN
    Goddess Athene, hear my prayer.

ACHILLES
    There isn't time for prayer. We have to move.

HELEN
Will I be rescued or killed?

ACHILLES
Which do you deserve?

HELEN
Why, will I be given what I what deserve, or will I deserve
what I'm given?

ACHILLES
That's too much of a riddle for a simple warrior.

HELEN
You are Achilles, son of Peleus.

ACHILLES
And you are Helen, wife of Menelaus. I'm to take you
to Agamemnon.

HELEN
I've dreamed of this day, and dreaded it.

ACHILLES
I'll escort you and stand by you.

HELEN
Let me finish my prayers.

ACHILLES
There isn't time. It isn't safe, for either of us.

HELEN
Goddess Athene, hear me. Grant me forgiveness, grant
me mercy. Goddess Athene, hear my prayers. Grant me
forgiveness and mercy.

ACHILLES
Helen . . .

*Achilles leans towards her and rests a hand on her shoulder.*
*Shot from a distance from Paris's bow, an arrow pierces*
*Achilles in the ankle, a fateful blow, pinning him to the*
*floor.*

PARIS
My brother's killer.

With my father's blood on his hands and his fist around
my wife's neck.

Was revenge ever so tellingly painted?

ACHILLES
Don't flatter yourself, Paris of the leopardskin cloak,
Paris of the fair skin and the silver tongue. My death
was written here, you're just the simple instrument.

PARIS
But what music, homicidal Achilles, destroyer of
families, scourge of life. What wonderful music.

ACHILLES
I hear it too, and I welcome it.

*Paris takes Achilles' sword from its sheath and hacks off*
*Achilles' foot. He holds the boot in the air then throws it*
*aside.*

PARIS
Stand up, Helen.

*Helen stands and faces Paris.*

Ten years you've slept in my bed. But what am I to you?
Husband, jailer, lover, partner in crime? You've never
said, and I've never asked.

*Agamemnon approaches slowly and calmly from a distance, visible to Helen but not to Paris.*

Which way your heart leans – you've never said. If love's needle points east or west.

Are you still a Greek, married to Menelaus, waiting for this day? Say so and you can run into the arms of the Greek army, disappear through that forest of shields and swords back to your old life.

Or are you mine? If that's how you feel we can still escape. Or die together in Troy, and be buried here.

Decide now, I'm offering the choice.

Say what you choose, Helen. There's no more time.

*Agamemnon stabs him in the back with a dagger. Paris dies.*

*Standing before her, Agamemnon raises his sword above Helen's head. From her statuesque form Athene reaches forward and removes Helen's headscarf, revealing and unfurling a long flowing mane of red hair.*

*Agamemnon gazes at her.*

AGAMEMNON
Helen of Sparta. My brother's wife. One of our own.

## SCENE TWELVE

*Troy. Present day.*

**Hera**

Still hanging around here? I should have known.

**Zeus**

Where else would I go?

**Hera**

What about Olympus? We haven't been there for ages.
How about a long weekend?

**Zeus**

Too cold for these old bones now. And too much of a
climb. I can't scale those heights any more.

**Hera**

People walk up it for fun these days. Hikers, day-trippers,
sightseers. There's probably a café at the summit.

**Zeus**

Ah, nothing's sacred, Hera. Everything's trampled on.

**Hera**

You live in the past.

**Zeus**

Live in the past? Of course I live in the past. I ruled over
the cosmos once, now look at me, a glorified beggar,
seller of knick-knacks and souvenirs.

Sometimes I wish I could die. We thought it was a
blessing – immortality. It never crossed my mind it was
a curse.

**Hera**

Well, you have an eternity to get used to it.

**Zeus**

Such power. Do you remember, Hera, how powerful
I was?

**Hera**

Masterful, Zeus. Quite masterful.

**Zeus**

It was a divine right. Handed down.

**Hera**

You slung your father into the burning fires of the
underworld – it was hardly a smooth succession.

**Zeus** (*gleefully*)

I did, I did. And do you remember how *he* overthrew *his*
father?

**Hera**

Another murder, was it?

**Zeus**

Lopped off his bollocks with a scythe! Those were the
days.

**Hera**

A very classy family I married into.

**Zeus**

But I had a softer side as well, didn't I? A bit of a
romantic on occasions?

**Hera**

You had your moments.

**Zeus**

Remember how we met? How I courted you?

**Hera**

Courted – that's an old-fashioned word.

**Zeus**
Wooed you.

**Hera**
Wooed? You're so ancient.

**Zeus**
Tell me you remember how we met.

**Hera**
You appeared as a bird.

**Zeus**
No just any bird.

**Hera**
A cuckoo. With a damaged wing.

**Zeus**
A poor little cuckoo with a broken wing. The illusion was quite astonishing.

**Hera**
Then flapped about at my feet. So to keep you warm I lifted you into my arms.

**Zeus**
To your breast, Hera. Lifted me to your breast. And the rest, as they say, is history.

**Hera**
In fact these days they say it's mythology.

*Pause.*

**Zeus**
Maybe if I'd leaned more the other way, to the Trojan side . . .

**Hera**
Let it go.

**Zeus**

Tell me my family didn't get involved while I slept. That it wasn't Athene who opened the gates of Troy, or your fist holding the hilt of Agamemnon's knife. I've always had my suspicions. Didn't I warn what would happen if we interfered?

**Hera**

New countries, new gods. The world turns. Literally, apparently – they say it's round.

**Zeus**

I knew that. I used to roll it around in the palm of my hand. I knew that all along.

**Hera**

There's a tour bus coming over the hill. Bring your mementoes and relics – we'll eat tonight.

*Hera exits.*

**Zeus**

Zeus. Selling plastic models of Zeus. Stood on a box dressed as a statue of Zeus, with a sign at his feet, saying 'Zeus'.

Give me a minute.

How many days for the fires to die down and the smoke to clear? Seven? Eight? The Trojan women branded with hot irons or the blades of swords, then chained. Not a Trojan man left alive. Not a child's voice. Greeks scurry like ants, fetching, carrying, loading the ships.

A blood-coloured river

runs down to the sea

between west and east.

## SCENE THIRTEEN

*Troy. The aftermath of the battle. Amidst the ruins of the sacked city the Greeks are preparing to leave. Odysseus is doing much of the organising, following Agamemnon's instructions. Helen is sitting on a packed sea-chest.*

AGAMEMNON
I trust you're happy with your share of the profits, Odysseus.

ODYSSEUS
The ships can't take any more. Any more and we'll sink.

AGAMEMNON
Then build rafts and tow them. We'll leave nothing here for the looters and treasure-hunters.

ODYSSEUS
A pity we had to be so destructive. This would have made a good outpost on the eastern front. Or a sovereign's winter home, Agamemnon?

AGAMEMNON
I'll never set foot in this flyblown wasteland again. Let's content ourselves with more riches than a man could dream of and the complete annihilation of the enemy race.

ODYSSEUS
The men are still emptying the vaults and the armoury. The wealth seems bottomless.

AGAMEMNON
Well, don't stop excavating till you hit the bedrock. When can we sail?

ODYSSEUS
  High tide is mid-afternoon.

AGAMEMNON
  See that we're fully loaded.

  Home, Odysseus. What's your wife called?

ODYSSEUS
  Penelope.

AGAMEMNON
  Oh yes, I knew that. Pretty name. And you've a boy, too,
  haven't you?

ODYSSEUS
  A babe in arms when I left. He won't know me.

AGAMEMNON
  We'll all have a lot of catching up to do. A lot of talking.
  (*Towards Helen.*) Explaining. (*To Helen.*) My brother
  waits for you by his vessel. I thought he'd be eager to
  see you after ten years; seems like he's busy stowing the
  valuables first. The delicate ornaments. The beautiful
  jewels.

ODYSSEUS
  What of the bodies?

AGAMEMNON
  Strip the armour from the enemy – we'll melt it down
  and work it again in our own fashion. Pile up the Trojan
  corpses and set fire to them. There's no time for digging
  graves.

ODYSSEUS
  And Achilles?

AGAMEMNON

A dignified funeral, I think, a few words. A burial stone
on the headland, perhaps.

ODYSSEUS

We should bear him home. Give his body back to his
father.

AGAMEMNON

It's an honourable notion!

And a right one. He'll have a hero's welcome, for the
part that he played in his king's victory. See that it
happens.

ODYSSEUS

I'll do that.

AGAMEMNON

And I want the ships scrubbed and the sails washed.
We're returning as heroes, Odysseus. I want us to dazzle.

*Odysseus and Agamemnon exit.*

*Filthy, bruised, in torn and tattered clothes, Andromache
crawls out from the ruins.*

HELEN

Andromache.

ANDROMACHE

You're going home. Helen of Sparta all along.

HELEN

Where is your son?

*Andromache shakes her head.*

HELEN
   I could take you with me.

ANDROMACHE
   To do what, comb your hair, fill your bath, hold your
   silk robes while you dress?

HELEN
   I'd make sure you were safe.

ANDROMACHE
   I couldn't promise the same. If you stood before me with
   your back turned. What might I do with a razor shell
   from your bedside table? Or a tight necklace?

*Andromache takes off her necklace, her only remaining*
*jewellery, and places it over Helen's head.*

HELEN
   What, then?

ANDROMACHE
   I want to stay here.

*Helen opens the sea-chest and takes out the tapestry. She*
*beckons Andromache to lie on it, then rolls it up with*
*Andromache inside.*

*Enter Odysseus.*

ODYSSEUS
   Unpacking? Packing? Unpacking?

HELEN
   There isn't room for this.

ODYSSEUS
   What is it?

HELEN
A tapestry. Ten years' worth.

ODYSSEUS
I'm sure we can find a place for it.

HELEN
I don't want it.

ODYSSEUS
But if you've put all that work into it.

HELEN
Leave it.

Would you disobey a queen of Greece?

ODYSSEUS
As you command.

HELEN
It tells a story – whoever finds it will know what happened here.

ODYSSEUS
Who needs a tapestry – open your eyes. These ruined palaces and piles of bones tell their own story.

HELEN
One side of it.

ODYSSEUS
The dead don't get to write the history books. That privilege belongs to the triumphant. To the living.

HELEN
I'm alive. Does that make me triumphant?

*Pause.*

**ODYSSEUS**

Look at those ships – they're so stuffed with gold and silver they're barely afloat.

Do you really think Greece risked its life to haul home an unfaithful wife?

**AGAMEMNON** (*off*)

Who's dawdling? The waves won't wait for any man. Not even Agamemnon.

**ODYSSEUS**

The horse wasn't made out of wood and nails, it was real – made out of flesh and blood. You opened the gates of Troy. My queen.

We sail on the tide.

*Odysseus exits, taking the last of the crates but leaving the tapestry.*

*In Greek, Helen sings her sad 'Song of the Lonely Wives' and exits towards the boats.*

*End of Act Two.*


THE END